The Virginia Militia in the Seventeenth Century

The Virginia Militia in the Seventeenth Century

William L. Shea

Louisiana State University Press
Baton Rouge and London

Manufactured in the United States of America

Designer: Albert Crochet
Typeface: Linotron Trump Mediaeval
Typesetter: Graphic Composition, Inc.
Printer: Thomson-Shore, Inc.
Binder: John H. Dekker & Sons, Inc.

Publication of this book has been assisted by a grant from the Andrew W. Mellon Foundation.

LIBRARY OF CONGRESS CATALOGING IN PUBLICATION DATA

Shea, William L.
The Virginia militia in the seventeenth century.

Bibliography: p.
Includes index.
1. Virginia—History, Military. 2. Virginia—Militia—History. 3. Virginia—History—Colonial period, ca. 1600–1775. I. Title.
F229.S53 1983 975.5'02 83-770
ISBN 0-8071-1106-6

for Pooh

Contents

Maps

Preface and Acknowledgments

American military history began with the establishment of colonial militias in the seventeenth century, but developments during this formative period generally have been overshadowed by the imperial and revolutionary struggles of the eighteenth century. To date only a handful of historians have examined the early colonial militias, and until now no full-length studies of seventeenth-century Anglo-American military institutions have appeared. This account of the Virginia militia is, therefore, a pioneering effort in a largely untilled field of Anglo-American history.

I have tried to write, as far as the surviving records permit, the story of the origin and evolution of the early Virginia militia. A rough chronological framework is provided by a narrative of the militia's role in several major Indian wars, a civil war, and numerous lesser crises. The changing nature of the militia as an institution is illustrated by examining its organization, composition, effectiveness, political reliability, tactics, equipment, and the like. Finally, the relationship between the militia and its parent society is explored by assessing the impact on the militia of the uncertain social, economic, and political conditions that plagued the Old Dominion during the seventeenth century. Despite the difficulties caused by enormous gaps in the records, a problem all too familiar to historians of early Virginia, I hope that readers will gain a better understanding of the manner in which the first successful English colonists perceived and dealt with the complex problems of security facing them in the New World.

I am especially indebted to Ira D. Gruber for his support and encouragement during the preparation of this book. I am also grateful to Sanford W. Higginbotham, William F. Droessler, Thad W. Tate, and Paul M. Graham, who provided advice and assistance during the past few years. Edward M. Riley and the Colonial Williamsburg Foundation generously tendered financial aid two years in a row, which allowed me to work for an extended period with the unparalleled resources and the unfailingly polite and professional staff of the Colonial Williamsburg Research Center. Finally, I owe special thanks to Pam Murphy for typing the manuscript more than once with matchless skill.

January 1 is considered the beginning of the year but Old Style dates are used throughout the book. A portion of Chapter 4 appeared in a slightly different form in *Military Affairs* as "Virginia at War, 1644–1646." Editor Robin Higham and the American Military Institute kindly permitted me to include that material here.

Abbreviations Used in the Notes

Archives	Brown, *Archives of Maryland*
BP	Blathwayt Papers
Collections	"Aspinwall Papers," Massachusetts Historical Society *Collections*
CO	Colonial Office Series
CP	Sir Henry Coventry Papers
EP	Baron Howard of Effingham Papers
EJC	McIlwaine and Hall, *Executive Journals of the Council of Colonial Virginia*
Genesis	Brown, *Genesis of the United States*
JHB	McIlwaine and Kennedy, *Journals of the House of Burgesses of Virginia*
JV	Barbour, *Jamestown Voyages Under the First Charter*
LJC	McIlwaine, *Legislative Journals of the Council of Colonial Virginia*
Minutes	McIlwaine, *Minutes of the Council and General Court of Colonial Virginia*
Narratives	Andrews, *Narratives of the Insurrections*
RVCL	Kingsbury, *Records of the Virginia Company of London*
Statutes	Hening, *Statutes at Large*
Tracts	Force, *Tracts and Other Papers*
TW	Arber and Bradley, *Travels and Works of Captain John Smith*
WBP	William Blathwayt Papers

The Virginia Militia in the Seventeenth Century

Introduction

American military history begins in seventeenth-century Virginia, but its roots lie a thousand years earlier in the great fyrd of Anglo-Saxon England. The great fyrd was more an abstract ideal than an actual military organization and might best be described as the concept of the nation in arms. The basis of the fyrd was the traditional obligation of every member of society to participate in the common defense. It was composed theoretically of every able-bodied freeman in the realm who could be summoned by the king in times of crisis to defend hearth and home against an invader. The fyrd was impermanent and intensely local. In most cases freemen took up arms to defend their shire only for as long as a threat existed. Despite these limitations Anglo-Saxon rulers relied heavily on the fyrd to supplement the tiny royal army of warriors and mercenaries. Portions of the fyrd fought in almost every major battle of which record exists, and the fyrdmen of Sussex struggled unsuccessfully with their king at Hastings in 1066 to repulse the Norman invasion.[1]

The victorious Normans were impressed with the fyrd and retained it as the foundation of their amalgamated Anglo-Norman military system. During the twelfth and thirteenth centuries a series of royal ordinances transformed the fyrd into a better organized, better armed, and more equitable force, henceforth known as the militia. Unfortunately, these ordinances could not preserve the martial pride and tribal loyalty that had infused the ancient fyrd. As the centuries passed the militia began to deteriorate, a decline accelerated when later medieval kings altered its role to fit their changing needs. England was more often the invader than the invaded after the Norman conquest, and the medieval militia gradually came to be used primarily as a source of manpower for overseas expeditions.[2]

1. Hollister, *Anglo-Saxon Military Institutions*, 7–37, and *Military Organization*, 3, 15–16; Smail, "Art of War," 130–33.

2. Hollister, *Anglo-Saxon Military Institutions*, 57–58, 128, 144–45, and *Military Organization*, 10–11, 219–20, 231–32; Smail, "Art of War," 139; Powicke, *Military*

In the sixteenth century Europe experienced a "military revolution" as compact, disciplined forces equipped with firearms were organized and made obsolete methods of warfare which had endured for a millennium. The growing threat of a Spanish invasion in the 1570s caused Elizabethan military leaders to look closely at what was happening on the Continent and to remodel the moribund English militia accordingly. They concluded, perhaps too hastily, that it was impossible to prepare every able-bodied man in the kingdom for modern warfare and decided instead to select a relatively small number of men in each shire—about one-tenth of the whole—and drill them in the latest military tactics. Elizabeth distrusted the peasantry and insisted that the men chosen for special duty be from the middling or better classes whenever possible. This "bourgeois militia," as one historian has termed it, was formed into small units called trainbands, literally trained bands. The remaining nine-tenths of the military population, poorly armed and ill trained, was relegated to the status of an inactive general reserve to be mobilized only in cases of extreme emergency.[3]

The trainbands usually received instruction in the art of war several times a year though the practice varied according to time and place. Command of these units belonged to willing members of the local gentry, but training was carried out under the watchful eyes of veteran soldiers called muster-masters. These men drilled the troops, inspected their equipment, and prepared them for possible combat, much like modern-day noncommissioned officers in a basic training program. The troops were expected to provide some of their own equipment but could borrow items as needed from the stocks of public and private weapons stored in town halls, parish churches, and castles all across the country. When fully decked out, trainbands presented a suitably martial appearance. Pikemen, still in vogue as a defense against cavalry, wore helmets and upper body armor, usually plate, and carried pikes. Musketeers normally wore a bit less armor and carried firearms, swords, and bandoliers. Most

---

Obligation, 50–54, 61, 166–81, 220–23; Beeler, *Warfare in Feudal Europe*, 100–119, 246.

3. Roberts, *Military Revolution*; Boynton, *Elizabethan Militia*, 16, 53, 90–96, 107–11; Cruickshank, *Elizabeth's Army*, 24, 287.

units also included a few horsemen armed with pistols, swords, and lances.[4]

The trainbands and general militia in each shire were placed under the control of an appointed official called the lord lieutenant, who was supposed to bring all his men together once or twice a year in a general muster. A gathering of the shire forces was a social as well as a military occasion in sixteenth-century England because it afforded everyone a welcome relief from the monotony of daily life. A typical general muster took place in a carnival atmosphere and lasted only one day. It usually included an inspection of men and arms, a formal review or mock battle, and an evening of merrymaking. The trainbands attended general musters primarily to participate in the festivities, though the men may also have welcomed an opportunity to demonstrate their martial prowess. Such affairs were entertaining but accomplished little except to reaffirm the widely held belief that the mass of the militia was useless.[5]

Such was the state of the English militia on the eve of colonization. A small minority of the adult male population had an opportunity to become amateur soldiers, and some undoubtedly achieved a certain level of competence, but the vast majority of Englishmen no longer had a meaningful role to play in their own defense. Whatever the strengths and weaknesses of the Elizabethan militia, it endured in one form or another for well over a century, gradually assuming a constabulary or domestic peacekeeping role in the tumultuous decades during and after the Civil War.[6]

Most of the Englishmen who traveled to Virginia at the beginning of the seventeenth century had no military experience beyond what little they had picked up in the Elizabethan militia, though a few were professional soldiers who had served in Ireland or on the Continent. Thus it is not surprising that they eventually settled on a militia as the most appropriate form of defense for their little outpost in the wilderness. But they did not slavishly copy what

4. Boynton, *Elizabethan Militia*, 23–25, 97–107; Cruickshank, *Elizabeth's Army*, 111–13; French, "Arms and Military Training," 3–21.

5. Thompson, *Lords Lieutenants*, 12–13, 45–51, 76–79; Boynton, *Elizabethan Militia*, 16–31; Cruickshank, *Elizabeth's Army*, 134, 193, 287.

6. Falls, *Elizabeth's Irish Wars*, 40–50; Boynton, *Elizabethan Militia*, 205–71; Western, *English Militia*, 50–51.

they had left behind. The constant danger posed by the Indians and other European powers caused the colonists to reject for nearly a century the contemporary English notion of a small, select militia and to turn instead to the concept of the nation in arms. As a result, they created in the New World a paramilitary institution remarkably like the great fyrd of ancient times. What follows is the story of this first Anglo-American militia.

1. False Starts and Failed Experiments

The Virginia Company of London was a commercial enterprise whose stockholders hoped to establish a settlement in North America which would provide them with a suitable return on their investment. Whether that return would be in the form of precious metals or a new route to the Orient was uncertain, but such an undertaking in an unknown land was clearly dangerous. Not surprisingly, nearly half of the instructions delivered to the colonists on the eve of their departure from England dealt with security. Company officials assumed that the Spanish would react quickly to the English intrusion in the New World and advised the colonists to select a strong site as far upriver as possible. Therefore, the instructions explained, if the Spanish were forced to search for the settlement "a hundred miles within the Land in boats you shall from both sides of your River where it is narrowest So beat them with Your muskets as they shall never be Able to prevail Against You." As an added precaution, a lookout post should be established at the mouth of the river to give the colonists sufficient warning of the approach of a Spanish fleet and prevent them from being surprised and destroyed as the French had been at Fort Caroline, a half century earlier in Florida.[1]

A settlement hidden in the interior might be relatively secure from European raiders, but it would be at the mercy of the surrounding Indians. Anglo-Indian relations had deteriorated rapidly at Sir Walter Raleigh's ill-fated settlements on Roanoke Island, the only previous English colonizing venture in the area. Recalling Raleigh's troubles, company officials suggested that the colonists adopt a cautious, defensive policy toward the natives, neither provoking them nor relying too heavily upon their goodwill. Trade for food with the Indians should be established before they realized the intruders planned to stay in their land, and if they were used as guides in explorations, they should not be trusted too far. They should

1. Craven, *Dissolution of the Virginia Company*, 24–29; "Instructions" [November or December, 1606], *JV*, I, 50; Quinn, *North America*, 240–61.

never be allowed to touch or carry guns lest they run away with them, leaving the colonists defenseless. Only the best marksmen should be allowed to shoot in front of the Indians, "for if they See Your Learners miss what they aim at they will think the Weapon not so terrible." The death of a settler should never be "advertised." Finally, the colonists were warned to prepare for the worst by maintaining a clear field of fire around the settlement. The instructions also emphasized that the Indians should be treated fairly with an eye toward future conversion to Christianity but assumed, at least for the present, that they were untrustworthy and possibly dangerous.[2]

Despite this explicit acknowledgment of the importance of military force as a means of self-defense, the Virginia Company did not have the financial resources to establish a mercenary army or any other formal, separate military organization. The company expected its employees in America to shoulder the burden of their own defense. Fighting, if required, was considered part of the job as well as a matter of self-preservation: each employee had a duty to participate in the defense of the enterprise. In this offhand manner something akin to the ancient Anglo-Saxon tradition of communal defense was transferred to the New World at the very beginning of the English colonial experience. It would become the basis of the early Virginia militia.

The Virginia expedition sailed from London in December, 1606, its three small ships crammed with more than one hundred colonists and several dozen sailors. Four months later, on April 26, 1607, the little fleet entered Chesapeake Bay. That evening a landing party splashed ashore near Cape Henry to have a look around and was fired on by a small band of Indians. Unsettled by the sharp engagement, the English quickly retired to their ships.[3] The natives, it seemed, were not very hospitable.

This skirmish at the water's edge reinforced the colonists' per-

2. "Instructions," *JV*, I, 50–52; Craven, "Indian Policy," 66–68; "Articles, Instructions, and Orders," November 20, 1606, *JV*, I, 43.

3. *TW*, I, cxxix; George Percy, "Observations gathered out of a Discourse of the Plantation of the Southerne Colonie in Virginia by the English, 1606" [n.d.], *JV*, I, 133–34; John Smith, *A True Relation of such occurrences and accidents of noate as hath hapned in Virginia since the first planting of that Collony* (London, 1608), *JV*, I, 170.

ception of the natives as inherently hostile. As they warily explored the bay and the James River in search of a landing site, the English met numerous Indians and visited some of their villages. Though these people were almost uniformly friendly, the English saw villainy at every hand. In this defensive frame of mind the first order of business was to establish a secure base camp. The settlers were pleased with a site they called Archer's Hope, noting that it "was sufficient with a little labour to defend our selves against any Enemy." But the water was too shallow there for the ships, and the English moved a little further upstream to an even more defensible site: a marshy peninsula connected to the mainland by a narrow neck. There, on May 14, they began to establish Jamestown. In doing so they ignored the part of their instructions which specifically prohibited settling "in a low and moist place because it will prove unhealthful."[4] Jamestown was chosen as the site for the base camp primarily because of its defensive properties: the neck of the peninsula could be fortified against the Indians, there was a clear view far downstream, and ships could tie up along the shore. To the little group of Englishmen alone in the wilderness of the New World, the peninsula offered security, if little else.

As the settlers unloaded supplies and set up their camp, they were visited by curious Indians from the nearby Paspehegh tribe. The Paspeheghs were friendly at first, but the English treated them with such ill-disguised suspicion and contempt that the insulted natives decided to eliminate the intruders. Choosing a time when many of the colonists were exploring upriver, several hundred Paspeheghs launched "a very furious Assault" upon the settlers at Jamestown and nearly overwhelmed them. The attackers would have surged inside the unfinished camp, which was protected only by a tangle of branches and felled trees, but for a handful of officers who defended the entrance passage. Edward Wingfield, president of the council and leader of the colony, "shewed himselfe a valiant Gentleman" in that desperate clash and had an arrow "shott cleane through his bearde, yet scaped hurte." The fight "indured hott about an hower" until the Indians were driven off by a barrage of musket

4. [Gabriel Archer], "A relatyon of the Discovery of our River" [May and June, 1607], *JV*, I, 82–95; Percy, "Observations," *ibid.*, I, 135–38; "Instructions," *ibid.*, I, 52.

and artillery fire from the three ships tied up along the shore. One English boy was killed and a dozen settlers and sailors injured.[5] All in all, it was a very near thing. Jamestown and its blundering inhabitants had been saved by Captain Christopher Newport's mariners. Had Archer's Hope with its shallow water been selected as the site for the camp, the story of the Virginia colony might have ended abruptly.

The unsuccessful attack on Jamestown marked the beginning of a period of chronic hostility that lasted until 1614, seven years of intermittent warfare consisting mainly of raids, skirmishes, and ambushes. At first the English acted defensively in accordance with their instructions. They quickly replaced the flimsy breastwork of branches with a stout fortification. "With all speede we pallisadoed our Fort," recalled one officer, and by mid-June the settlers had completed a large triangular structure with walls about fifteen feet high, "having three Bulwarkes at every corner like a halfe Moone, and foure or five pieces of Artillerie mounted in them." Each semicircular bulwark or raised gun platform contained a variety of cannon ranging from sizable culverins and demiculverins to smaller antipersonnel weapons such as sakers and falcons.[6]

In the beginning the English were continually harassed by the Paspeheghs, but the natives became reluctant to approach the ships and the fort once they were armed with impressive weapons. For a time they contented themselves with hiding in the woods and flinging volleys of arrows toward the settlers. On one occasion they "shott above 40 arrowes into, and about the forte," causing no harm but sparking a mad scramble for cover. Within a few days, however, a more deadly pattern of snipings and ambushes emerged. One Sunday morning some Paspeheghs "came lurking in the thicketes and long grasse" near the fort. An unsuspecting colonist wandered out and was struck with six arrows. He staggered back into the compound "crying Arme Arme," yet to the surprise of the English,

5. Percy, "Observations," *ibid.*, 139–41; [Archer], "Relatyon," *ibid.*, I, 95; John Smith, *A Map of Virginia. With a Description of the Countrey, the Commodities, People, Government and Religion* (Oxford, 1612), *ibid.*, II, 379–80.

6. Smith, *True Relation*, *ibid.*, I, 172; Smith, *Map of Virginia*, *ibid.*, II, 379–80; Percy, "Observations," *ibid.*, I, 142; Lewis, "Armada Guns," 62–69.

"the Salvages stayed not, but run away." A few days later several Indians crept up to one of the bulwarks at dawn and spotted a colonist "goeing out to doe naturall necessity." They killed him and again withdrew unscathed. Like incidents began to occur almost daily, and the settlers found themselves besieged. Captain John Smith observed that the English "by their disorderly stragling were often hurt, when the Salvages by the nimblenesse of their heeles well escaped."[7] Bottled up within Jamestown and mystified by the Indians' irregular tactics, the English were beginning their conquest of North America from a difficult position.

Their situation steadily worsened throughout 1607 and into the following year. The colonists were unable to hunt, fish, or farm effectively and came to rely almost exclusively on their uncertain supply line to England. This was a disastrous mistake for supply ships arrived infrequently and carried more settlers than commodities. Dwindling food supplies led to malnutrition, and diseases ravaged the population. Morale plummeted. "There were never Englishmen left in a forreigne Countrey in such miserie as wee were in this new discovered Virginia," wailed George Percy. Under such wretched conditions discontent flourished and authority broke down. Effective leadership collapsed as members of the council deposed Wingfield and squabbled among themselves. The fort and the thatched huts within were burned in midwinter and had to be rebuilt, but the precious stores consumed by the flames could not be replaced. Sick, weak, leaderless, and nearly bereft of supplies, the shrinking band of Englishmen struggled to hang on, "not having five able men to man our Bulwarkes upon any occasion."[8] For the first but not the last time the Virginia colony tottered on the edge of collapse.

Ironically, the Indians saved the English from their own ineptitude during this period. The expedition had landed in an area dominated by Powhatan, a powerful Indian leader whose empire, the so-called Powhatan confederation, included most of tidewater Virginia. Powhatan eventually halted hostilities for a time, possibly

7. [Archer], "Relatyon," *JV*, I, 95–97; Smith, *Map of Virginia, ibid.*, II, 380.

8. Percy, "Observations," *ibid.*, I, 142–45; Smith, *Map of Virginia, ibid.*, II, 385, 393; Earle, "Environment, Disease, and Mortality," 96–125.

because he believed that the Europeans and their powerful weapons could be enlisted in the struggle to expand his empire. Observing the increasingly hapless state of the settlement, Powhatan instructed his people to keep the strangers alive until he could decide their fate. The English knew little of these machinations and were amazed to find the Indians bringing them small amounts of food, sometimes in exchange for metal implements, sometimes as a gift. They understandably attributed their salvation to divine intervention rather than to a whim on Powhatan's part. A perplexed Captain Smith pondered how "it pleased God (in our extremity) to move the Indians to bring us Corne . . . to refresh us, when we rather expected they would destroy us."[9]

But Smith was not a man to wallow long in despair or depend on handouts from savages. He took over as president of the colony in September, 1608, sixteen months after the founding of Jamestown. Smith's brief and celebrated reign was notable for his strong leadership and his attempts to instill discipline and military training into the colonists in pursuit of an aggressive policy to intimidate the Indians. Smith was by trade a mercenary, a soldier of fortune, a veteran of assorted European conflicts who was fascinated by novel military situations. The strategy and tactics he advocated remained the standard in Virginia long after his departure.[10]

The captain was dismayed by the absence of experienced soldiers in Virginia. He denounced the colonists as "being for most part of such tender educations and small experience in martiall accidents" as to be virtually useless as soldiers. He noted that during the Paspehegh attacks on Jamestown there were numerous settlers "not knowing what to doe, nor how to use a Piece." The widespread lack of military training may have meant that many of the settlers had belonged to the general reserve back home or had avoided militia service altogether. Their helplessness was intolerable, and Smith took advantage of the continuing lull in the fighting to prepare his untrained men for the next round. The twice-built fort was rebuilt once again, this time in the shape of a pentagon. Block-

9. Lurie, "Indian Cultural Adjustment," 33–60; Smith, *True Relation*, *JV*, I, 173.
10. *TW*, II, 433. The standard biography is Barbour, *Three Worlds of Captain John Smith*.

houses were constructed and garrisoned near the neck of the peninsula, sentry details were trained and posted for set watches, and "the whole Company every Saturday exercised, in the plaine by the west Bulwarke, prepared for that purpose, we called Smithfield: where sometimes more then an hundred Salvages would stand in an amazement to behold, how a fyle would batter a tree, where [Smith] would make them a marke to shoot at." Smith went beyond a static defense of Jamestown. Reasoning that he could best secure the fort by maintaining pressure on the enemy, the captain prepared some of his men "to march, fight, and scirmish" in the forests of the New World. After a week of intensive training Smith was satisfied that his amateur soldiers could establish an "order of battle amongst the Trees" strong enough to withstand anything Powhatan could throw against them.[11]

But the lack of military experience was only part of the problem; equally serious was the erosion of authority in the floundering colony, and the captain struggled to instill discipline into his troops. Smith divided the lolling English into work gangs and moved to halt the "disorderly stragling" that had cost so many lives. He attempted to stop the flow of equipment to the Indians that threatened to ruin the colony. In return for baskets of food, shortsighted settlers already had traded away "the most part of our tooles, and a good part of our Armes," including three hundred axes and hatchets, fifty swords, eight muskets, pikes, powder, shot, and assorted other metal implements. A few colonists even acceded to Powhatan's request to teach his warriors how to use firearms. The Indians also made off with whatever they could carry, sometimes actually wresting tools or arms away from settlers walking outside the fort.[12] Within a short time Smith was able to beat, bully, and threaten his own people more or less into line, securing the fort in preparation for whatever might happen when he turned his attention toward the Indians.

Captain Smith had become disenchanted with the Virginia Com-

11. Smith, *True Relation*, *JV*, I, 202; Smith, *Map of Virginia*, *ibid.*, II, 373; *TW*, II, 433–34.

12. *TW*, II, 388, 441, 466–67; Smith, *True Relation*, *JV*, I, 200; Smith, *Map of Virginia*, *ibid.*, II, 430; Fausz, "Fighting 'Fire' with Firearms," 33–50.

pany's cautious policy toward the Indians, and now "he made bold to try such conclusions as necessitie inforced, though contrary to his Comission." As the uneasy truce between the Indians and the English began to break down, Smith resolved to seize the initiative, regardless of past instructions or future consequences. By this time the captain had become familiar with Indian methods of warfare. Powhatan's fighting men wore no armor except small shields made of bark and usually carried bows, clubs, wooden swords, and iron hatchets (the last item acquired from the English). Formal, massed battles were rare. The natives preferred a stealthier game, stalking their antagonists in a loose, irregular manner in which "they scatter them selves sum litle distant one from the other" and "softly steale toward their enemies." After the initial attack on Jamestown they were reluctant to expose themselves to musket or artillery fire and sought cover behind trees and brush whenever possible. They delighted in picking off stragglers and ambushing unwary parties. All in all, Smith concluded, they relied heavily on "Strategems, trecheries, or surprisals."[13] Such a skilled, mobile, and numerous enemy would be very difficult to defeat or destroy; a resolute show of force, however, might overawe the Indians.

With Jamestown reasonably secure, Smith commenced a series of bold actions intended to cow Powhatan into submission and establish a steady supply of food as tribute rather than as charity. Armed with pistol, sword, and target, and accompanied by his "souldiers" with jacks and matchlock muskets, the captain soon succeeded in terrorizing Indian tribes up and down the James River. Powhatan returned guns and other stolen goods, and the English could boast that the natives "did know wee had such a commanding power at James towne they durst not wrong us of a pin." Perhaps the best indication of John Smith's control over balky settlers and natives occurred during the summer of 1609, when an unexpected supply ship was mistaken for a Spanish intruder. One colonist recalled that Smith so quickly "determined and ordered our

13. *TW*, II, 364, 367, 393; Henry Spelman, "Relation of Virginea" [1613], *ibid.*, I, cxiii–cxiv.

affaires, as we little feared their Arrivall, nor the successe of our incounter; nor were the Salvages any way negligent for the most part, to ayd and assist us with their best power."[14] The sight of Englishmen and Indians jointly poised to resist an invader was a far cry from the hostility of earlier days. But it was not to last.

The end of a brief era came in the fall of 1609, when Smith was badly burned in the explosion of a powder charge ignited by the smoldering match of his musket. He soon took ship for England, reflecting that "it was his ill chance to end, when he had but onely learned how to begin." He could take some comfort knowing that the beginning was apparently sound. The colony now held nearly five hundred persons, one hundred of them "well trayned and expert Souldiers," even by Smith's rigorous standards. The town was "strongly Pallizadoed" and contained twenty-four cannons, three hundred firearms, and more pikes, swords, and helmets than men to use them.[15] The Virginia project remained a poorly organized and underfinanced operation, but the energetic efforts of this one military strong man had reversed the slide toward oblivion.

Back in London the Virginia Company began to take steps to improve the colony's fortunes along the militant lines Smith had initiated: rigorous military training, rigid discipline, authoritarian leadership, and an aggressive policy toward the Indians. This new approach, known in modern terms as the "military regime," probably can best be understood as the second in a series of experiments in colonization by the company, part of a continuing effort to adjust theories and policies to fit the reality of the situation in America. The initial experiment that began in 1607 had failed. Hence the second experiment was modeled to some degree after contemporary English military expeditions to Ireland and the Low Countries. The Virginia project had to become stable and secure before it could become commercially viable, and John Smith had pointed

14. *TW*, II, 440, 393, 474, 479; Smith, *True Relation*, *JV*, I, 175, 191, 195, 204; Smith, *Map of Virginia*, *ibid.*, II, 395–96, 428, 410–44. A jack was a heavy quilted coat of cotton or canvas useful against stone-age weapons. A target was a small round shield made of wood or metal.

15. *TW*, II, 477, 484, 486.

the way. The military regime lasted in one form or another until 1619, and during those years the policies initiated by the pushy young captain were carried to their logical extreme.[16]

Unfortunately, shipwrecks and other problems caused a year's delay between Smith's departure and the establishment of the new administration. In the meantime, the situation in Virginia deteriorated. As one settler recalled, "The Salvages no sooner understood Smith was gone, but they all revolted, and did spoile and murther all they incountered." The colonists' military efforts were feeble and ineffective. Outposts were overrun. Foraging parties were ambushed. The interim president and more than thirty men were tricked by that "subtell oulde foxe" Powhatan into entering his village and were wiped out. Smith's work was quickly undone by incompetent leadership and lax discipline. Once again in a state of siege and now unable to beg or seize food from the Indians, the English entered the winter of 1609–1610, the terrible "starving time." When reinforcements finally reached Virginia in the summer of 1610 they found Jamestown a shambles, the Indians *"as fast killing without as the famine and pestilence within."* Huddled inside the decrepit fort were only sixty survivors.[17] The colony had nearly been exterminated, but a new and more militant beginning was at hand.

The leaders of this second phase of colonization were "excellent old soldiers" who had served with distinction in Ireland and "that university of warre" the Low Countries: Sir Thomas West (Lord De La Warr), Sir Thomas Gates, and Sir Thomas Dale. They naturally drew upon their previous experience in dealing with the situation in Virginia. Appalled by the disorderly and almost defenseless state of affairs at Jamestown, they moved to regiment the colonists and militarize the colony. The settlers were divided into "severall Companies for warr" with "Captaines appointed over every fifty to traine them at convenient times and to teache them the use of

16. Rutman, "Virginia Company," 1–20; Canny, *Elizabethan Conquest of Ireland,* 159–63.

17. Another forty survivors were recovered at Point Comfort. See *TW*, II, 497, 499; Percy, "Trewe Relacyon," 265, 270; Governor and Council to Virginia Company, July 7, 1610, *Genesis*, I, 404–405.

their armes and weapons" so that "they may knowe whether uppon all occasions and sudden attempts they shall repayre to find them in a readines." A military-style command structure quickly was established, and the settlers soon were being strenuously "exercised and trayned up in Martiall manner and warlike Discipline," further evidence that the great majority of Englishmen arriving in Virginia were not sufficiently schooled in the arts of war. When not drilling or performing military tasks these same companies served as work gangs that labored mightily cultivating crops, rebuilding Jamestown, and erecting new towns and facilities up and down the river.[18]

Virginia's military regime was unique in American history. Traditional English norms were replaced by a very different form of social organization: company, squadron, and file. Accepted English titles and ranks were replaced by a more rigid hierarchy: captain general, marshal, colonel, captain, lieutenant, ensign, sergeant, corporal, and private. Social status and privilege came to depend largely on a person's current military rank, not his English background, for the regime's famed *Lawes Divine, Morall and Martiall* decreed that "All Captaines shall command all Gentlemen, and Common Souldiers in their Companies, to obey their Sergeants, and Corporals, in their offices, without resisting, or injuring the said Officers."[19] A military hierarchy, or at least a hierarchy based on military organization and using military titles and nomenclature, was impressed on the formless aggregate of the early years. The problems of discipline and disorder which had plagued Smith and other early leaders were resolved temporarily. And yet in many ways the militarization of the colony was superficial. The martial atmosphere existing for a few years after 1610 did not alter the basic situation. Virginia was still a commercial enterprise, and the colonists were still employees of the Virginia Company. The dual role of each colonist as soldier and laborer remained unchanged,

18. Strachey, *Historie of Travell*, 90–91; John Pory to [Sir Dudley Carleton], September 30, 1619, *RVCL*, III, 220; "Instructions to La Warr" [February 28, 1609/10], *ibid.*, 24–29; "Instructions Orders and Constitutions," May, 1609, *ibid.*, 12–24.

19. Strachey, *For the Colony in Virginea Britannia. Lawes Divine*, 28, 83, 42–43, 46, 65, 72–73.

and though the former role was greatly expanded during the military regime, it did not wholly overshadow the latter. Each soldier-laborer continued to have a twofold duty: "to hold warre" and to do "the service requisite to the subsisting of a colonie."[20] The Virginian and, much later, southern fascination with military titles may have been one of the very few lasting effects of the military regime.

During the military regime the colonists were well drilled, fully equipped, and provided with competent leadership in the war against Powhatan. Everyone was required to learn the proper use and care of modern weapons. Because there were few survivors from Smith's regime and more recent arrivals had little or no military background, a training program was begun. Men usually drilled while on watch so the bulk of the population might labor in the fields without interruption. Guard duty rotated among the companies so that perhaps once a week each man put in a full day of marching, shooting, and practicing the manual of arms. Training concentrated on the use of firearms: "Officers shall teach every Souldier to handle his peece, first to present it comely, and souldier like, and then to give fire, by false firing, and so to fall his Piece to the right side with the nose up, and when their souldiers are hardy and expert in this, they shall set up a convenient mark fast by the court of Guard, at which every Souldier shall twice discharge his peece, at the releeving of the watch, morning and evening." The clumsy matchlock musket was the standard European firearm of the day and was the one most widely used in early Virginia. Soldiers drilled and sentries patrolled the ramparts of Jamestown with muskets shouldered and "Match in Cock." But the matchlock was being replaced by the snaphance musket, an early flintlock, which was lighter and easier to handle and thus better suited to American conditions.[21]

The settlers also were equipped with a considerable variety of other arms and implements. In 1611 the company obtained a large supply of obsolescent armor from the king and sent it to Virginia.

20. *Ibid.*, 83.
21. *Ibid.*, 45–46, 80; Peterson, *Arms and Armor*, 43, 98–99.

In John Smith's time the colonists had worn only helmets and jacks for protection. The new equipment gave them a much more formidable if somewhat medieval appearance. The military governors carefully instructed their officers to make sure that "every shot shall either be furnished with a quilted coate of Canvas, a head-peece, and a sword, or else with a light Armor, and Bases quilted, with which hee shall be furnished: and every Targiteer with his Bases to the small of his legge, and his headpeece, sword and pistoll, or Scuppet provided for that end. And likewisee every Officer armed as before, with a firelocke, or Snaphaunse, headpeece, and a Target, onely the Serjeant in Garrison shall use his Halbert, and in field his Snaphaunse and Target." All settlers, soldiers and officers alike, were required to wear their full complement of arms and armor while on guard duty so that they would not find the equipment so "uncouth, strange and troublesome" when in the field.[22]

The offensive operation or "march" was the most dangerous time for the early colonists because it meant that a relatively small group of men would be facing large numbers of hostile Indians far from the security of their base. Discipline was essential and was enforced with great severity. Settlers who deserted, lost their arms, ran away from a fight, or surrendered without permission were executed; those who straggled, wasted ammunition, or disobeyed lesser orders were punished brutally. Faced with such unpleasant alternatives, the soldier-laborers had little choice but to master the mysteries of marching, maneuvering, and fighting, both as single companies and as combined units. Progress apparently was rapid. The first of the military governors, Lord De La Warr, soon felt confident enough to launch a series of punitive raids against neighboring tribes.[23]

In August, 1610 De La Warr dispatched Captain George Percy and a reinforced company to smash the Paspeheghs. The redoubtable Percy, whom Smith called a man "of as bold resolute spirits as could possibly be found," produced an unusually detailed ac-

22. Percy, "Trewe Relacyon," 276; Strachey, *For the Colony . . . Lawes Divine*, 45–46; Peterson, *Arms and Armor*, 114–32. A scuppet was a pistol, and a base probably was either a jack or buff coat, a heavy leather garment much like a modern overcoat.

23. Strachey, *For the Colony . . . Lawes Divine*, 27–28, 34–35, 87.

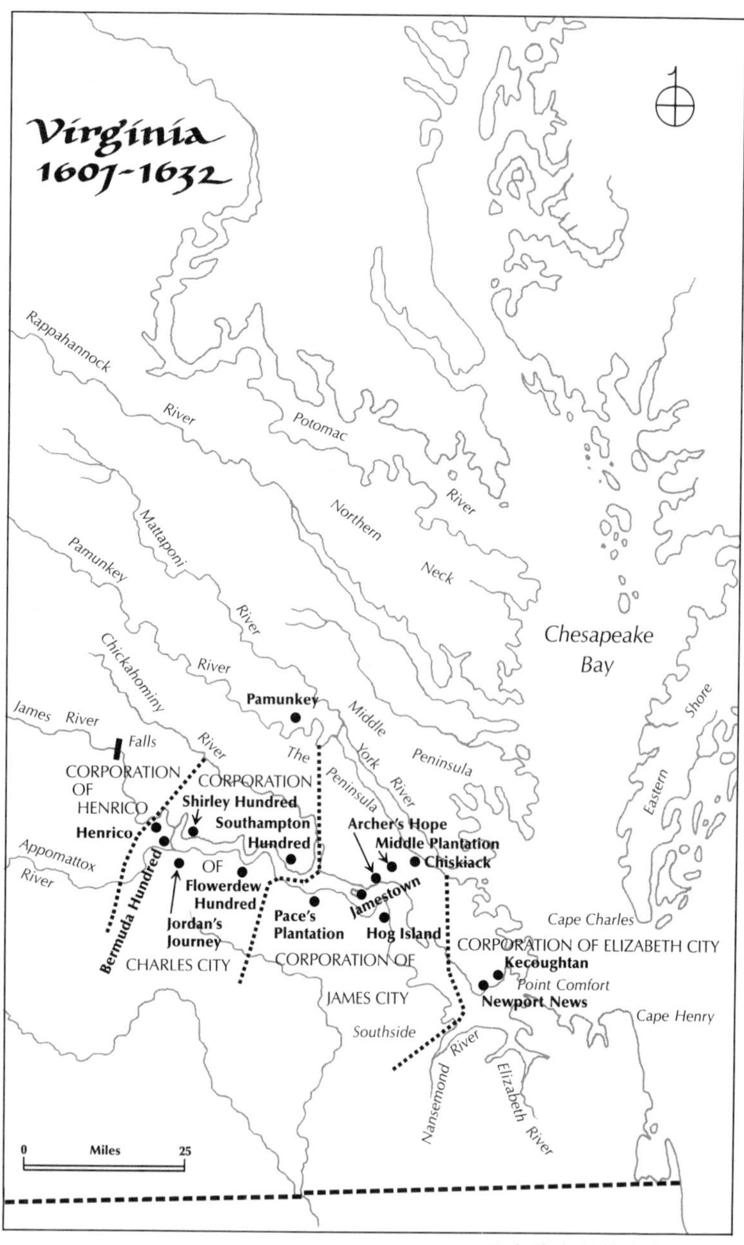

Map by Whitehead & Whitehead, Austin, Texas

count of this expedition, though his spelling and punctuation leave much to be desired. With seventy men in two boats, Percy sailed to within three miles of the main Paspehegh village above Jamestown and there landed his modest force.

> Then draweing my sowldiers into Battalio [and] placeing a Capteyne or Leftenante att every fyle we marched towards the Towne haveinge An Indyan guyde with me named Kempes whome the Provoste marshall ledd in A hande locke. This Subtell Salvage . . . browghte us the righte way near unto the Towne. So that then I Comawnded ever[y] Leader to drawe A way his fyle before me to besett the salvages houses thatt noene mighte escape with a chardge nott to geve the allarume untill I weare come upp unto them with the Cullers. At my comeinge I appointed Capte: William Weste to geve the Allarume the which he performed by shooteinge of a pistoll. And then we fell in upon them putt some fiftene or sixtene to the Sworde and Almoste all the reste to flyghte. Whereupon I cawsed my drume to beate and drewe all my Sowldiers to the Cullers. . . . And then dispersed my fyles Apointeinge my Sowldiers to burne their howses and to cutt downe their Corne groweinge aboutt the Towne. . . . Then sayleinge some towe myles downe the River I sentt Capte: Davis A shoare with Moste of my Sowldiers. . . . Capte: Davis att his landeinge was Apponted by some Indyans who spared nott to send their Arrowes amongste our men but within A shorte Tyme he putt them to flighte and landed withoutt further opposityon [and] marcheinge Aboutt fowrtene myles into the Cowntry cutt downe their Corne [and] burned their howses, Temples and Idolles. . . . So haveinge performed all the spoyle he could Retourned Aboarde to me ageine and then we sayled downe the River to James Towne.

Despite specific orders against taking prisoners, Percy found himself holding the Paspehegh queen and her two children after the battle. On the way back to Jamestown he bowed to pressure from his men and killed the children "by Throweinge them overboard and shoteinge owtt their Braynes in the water." The woman was killed shortly thereafter on De La Warr's orders.[24]

Meanwhile, other English raiding parties were at work downriver from Jamestown. Sir Thomas Gates, soon to replace the ailing De La Warr as governor, took a company to a small Indian town called Kecoughtan. Upon landing there he produced a taborer who

24. *TW*, II, 476; Percy, "Trewe Relacyon," 271–73.

played and danced before the fascinated—and distracted—natives. "And then espyeinge A fitteinge opportunety," Gates and his men "fell in upon them, putt fyve to the sworde, [and] wownded many others, some of them beinge after fownde in the woods with Sutche extreordinary Lardge and mortall wownds thatt itt seamed strange they Cold flye so far. The reste of the Salvages he putt to flighte." A fortified compound was erected to secure the fertile fields around the razed Indian village. Captain Samuel Argall led another company across the river against the Wariscoyacks, who fled at his approach. The English contented themselves with "Cutteinge downe their Corne, burneinge their howses, and Sutche lyke." These punitive operations came to be called "feedfights" because they were aimed at destroying Indian crops and stores of food. Such tactics proved devastatingly effective and became the standard English method of striking back at the Indians for the next forty years.[25]

The English stepped up their activities the following year. Sir Thomas Dale, the third of the military leaders, arrived in 1611 with three hundred additional men and large supplies of weapons, armor, and ammunition. Dale soon followed the example of his energetic predecessors by leading one hundred troops downriver to do battle with the Nansemond tribe. This time, the Indians fought furiously in defense of their village. Both company commanders were wounded, and Dale was struck "juste upon the edge or Brimme of his headpiece" by an arrow, "which if itt had fallen A thowght Lower mightt have Shott him into the Braynes and indangered his Lyfe." The natives performed "exorcismes, conjuracyons, and charmes, throweinge fyer upp into the skyes, [and] Runneinge up and downe with many irigramantcke Spelles and incantacionus" in an effort to overcome the colonists' armor and muskets. But technology triumphed over the supernatural; the Nansemonds were driven back, and their town and crops were destroyed.[26]

Raiding and skirmishing dragged on for the next three years. The English retained the initiative and were dominant in battle but failed to achieve a decisive victory or force their opponents to seek a truce.

25. Percy, "Trewe Relacyon," 270–73; Fausz and Kukla, "Letter of Advice," 126.
26. Percy, "Trewe Relacyon," 275–77.

Dale continued to lead sallies against the enemy and again "escaped killing very narrowly." Despite close calls, English casualties were light, undoubtedly the result of the increasing use of armor. The Indians had been put on the defensive and were reduced to occasional sniping. One settler observed that the only English losses during the military regime were the result of "folly and indiscreation" for the Indians caused few casualties "in Skirmish, fort or feild," other than setting traps for the unwary.[27]

As the war against the Indians gained momentum, the military leaders began to expand and strengthen the colony. Their first priority was to establish a new "principall Towne" deep in the interior that would be "an impregnable retreat, against any forraign invasion, how powerfull so ever." But although everyone was properly concerned about Spanish intentions, the immediate and ever-present danger remained the Indians. Hence Dale chose a site for the new town that was defensible against attack by sea or land. The town, to be called Henrico, was located atop a bluff almost completely surrounded by a loop of the James River. In 1611 Dale set 350 men to work erecting two parallel palisades across the narrow base or neck of this little riverine peninsula. The palisades were roughly two miles apart and were reinforced with blockhouses at regular intervals. Blockhouses also were located along the curving shoreline, and watchtowers were constructed at each corner of the new town, though the town itself was not enclosed with a pale. These precautions were taken to secure Henrico from Indian attacks; the location of the town probably was considered sufficient protection against a naval invasion. Dale drove his men mercilessly through the summer and fall. Within four months the settlers had finished the defensive works, numerous houses and storehouses, and a church and had made Henrico "much better and of more worth than all the worke ever since the Colonie began."[28]

The English soon established a complex of fortified settlements around Henrico. Coxendale, Rochdale, and Bermuda Hundred, like

27. Sir Samuel Argall to Nicholas Hawes, June, 1613, *Genesis*, II, 640; Strachey, *Historie of Travell*, 45, 64, 109.

28. Sir Thomas Dale to president and council, May 25, 1611, *Genesis*, I, 491; Hamor, *True Discourse*, 28–32.

Henrico, were located on riverine peninsulas separated from the Virginia mainland by wooden barriers two to four miles in length. The colonists had learned that the Indians were reluctant to attack fortified positions. Consequently, they began to erect palisades everywhere they went. While Dale hacked Henrico out of the wilderness, Gates turned his attention to Jamestown. A large area just east of the old fort was impaled and filled with houses and other structures. The west bulwark or bastion of the fort was raised, strengthened, and converted into a "faire platforme" for a full complement of artillery. Defenses along the neck of the peninsula were improved to reduce even further the possibility of Indian raids on the town. Virginia was more secure than ever before.[29]

Fortified and armored, the English were becoming resigned to a struggle of indefinite length when suddenly, in 1614, fighting came to an abrupt halt. Powhatan's daughter, Pocahontas, was lured aboard a small English vessel and carried off to Jamestown. The military leaders planned to hold her for ransom, but after a time the girl converted to Christianity and fell in love with a colonist named John Rolfe. The result was a match in the best tradition of European diplomacy. Ralph Hamor related how the pair were married in the little church at Jamestown with several Indian dignitaries in attendance, adding that "ever since we have had friendly commerce and trade, not onely with Powhatan himselfe, but also with his subjects round about us." Shortly afterward Dale led a company of "well appointed" troops to a peace conference with the Chickahominy Indians, who were independent of Powhatan. Like that chieftain, this "stout and warlike Nation" of five hundred bowmen agreed to become allies of the English and to support them against the Spanish. They also pledged to return stray cattle and not to harm Englishmen or their defensive works. The colonists in turn promised to protect the Chickahominies from their enemies.[30]

After seven years of sporadic violence the English had at last established a "firme peace" with the surrounding Indians. For a

29. Hamor, *True Discourse*, 30–33. The only other detailed accounts of military affairs in early Virginia are two dissertations: Rutman, "Militant New World," and Fausz, "Powhatan Uprising."

30. Hamor, *True Discourse*, 5–16, 55–57.

short time they cautiously kept up their guard against their new allies, but gradually the defensive posture of the colony began to soften. The military regime faded away as the ironfisted commanders returned to Europe, their particular services no longer needed. As it had done a decade earlier, the Virginia Company inaugurated yet another experiment in colonization, this one as civil as its predecessor had been militant. The emphasis now was on commercial expansion, for "the Colony beginneth now to have the face and fashion of an orderly State, and as such is likely to grow and prosper." In 1619 the new leader, Sir George Yeardley, formally replaced "the rigour of Martiall Law" with a new form of government consisting of a governor, council, assembly, and a number of lesser offices, none of them military.[31]

It is not surprising that military affairs and thoughts of self-defense were largely overlooked after 1614. The colonists were relieved that the long nightmare was over, glad to be rid of the excesses of the military regime, and preoccupied with making money from tobacco. Peace and the erosion of the strict discipline and rigid organization of the military regime allowed the settlers to do largely whatever they pleased, which usually was to concentrate on raising the colony's one cash crop. When Dale left Virginia in 1616 nearly everyone still lived and worked in an enforced communal fashion at a palisaded settlement. A year later the inhabitants were found to be "dispersed all about, planting *Tobacco*." As the population scattered many of the fortified garrison towns, secured with so much effort, were virtually abandoned. The fifty-man companies were dissolved, and military drill was discontinued. After all, when everyone could see the aged Powhatan going "from place to place visiting his Country taking his pleasure in good friendship with us," trouble with the natives seemed unlikely. The old chief died in 1618, but peaceful relations and English complacency continued.[32]

The famous assembly that met at Jamestown in 1619 to inau-

31. *Ibid.*, 2; *A Declaration of the State of the Colony and Affaires in Virginia* (London, 1620), *RVCL*, III, 310–11; Rutman, "Virginia Company," 20.

32. *TW*, II, 535, 539; Rolfe, *True Relation*, 4; Craven, *Dissolution of the Virginia Company*, 37–40; Morgan, *American Slavery*, 108–12.

gurate the new government mentioned the Indian problem only in passing and emphasized keeping the peace rather than preparing for war. Inhabitants were strictly directed not to injure or oppress the Indians "whereby the present peace might be disturbed and antient quarrells might be revived." Nothing was done to revitalize the promising paramilitary system which had fallen into decay after 1614. Men were no longer required to drill, train, assemble, or carry arms. Normal daily intercourse with the Indians was to continue without regulation or supervision. Looking back years later, after this lax state of affairs had led to disaster, a perplexed John Smith wrote: "It hath oft amazed me to understand how . . . the Salvages that doe little but continually exercise their bow and arrowes, should dwell and lie so familiarly amongst our men that practiced little but the Spade; being so farre asunder, and in such small parties dispersed, and neither Fort, exercise of armes used, Ordinances mounted, Courts of guard, nor any preparation nor provision to prevent a forraine enemy, much more the Salvages." From his vantage point in London the old soldier found it hard to believe that in Virginia men could ignore the danger all around them and go "rooting in the ground about Tobacco like Swine."[33] But that is exactly what they did.

33. John Pory, "A Reporte of the manner of proceeding in the general assembly convented at James City in Virginia, July 30, 1619," *RVCL*, III, 164–73; *TW*, II, 563; Morgan, *American Slavery*, 112.

2. A Massacre and a Militant Response

In 1621 Sir Francis Wyatt was dispatched to Virginia to replace George Yeardley as governor. Soon after his arrival Wyatt learned that rumors of Indian unrest were circulating around the colony. He also learned that the settlers were not particularly alarmed because in the past they had experienced "many the like Alarumes which cam to nothinge." The new governor, fresh from Europe and aware of his lack of knowledge about the natives, decided to learn what they were up to. He contacted Powhatan's successor, Opechancanough, and demanded to know if there was any truth to the rumors. The chief denied any hostile intentions and earnestly declared that "the Skye should sooner falle then Peace be broken" on his part. Wyatt was satisfied that Opechancanough was committed to peace and turned his attention to other business.[1]

Unfortunately, Wyatt had been deceived. Indian grievances had been mounting since the Rolfe-Pocahontas marriage seven years earlier. The two basic problems were a lack of space and cultural incompatibility. In their quest for tobacco profits the English had been expropriating agricultural land at a rapid rate along the James River, and the Virginia Company recently had intensified its clumsy but well-meaning campaign to convert the Indians to Christianity and acculturate them to English ways. Threatened on two vital fronts, by 1621 Opechancanough and his people had become greatly alarmed and were primed for an explosion. Then Nemattanew, the "chiefe Captaine" of the Pamunkeys, murdered a settler and was in turn killed. His loss enraged the Indians and led them to plan a shattering revenge that would sweep the newcomers away forever. Opechancanough's vow of peace to Wyatt was made amidst preparations for war.[2]

In the predawn darkness of March 22, 1622, the inhabitants of

1. Council to Virginia Company, January, 1621/2 and January 20, 1622/3, *RVCL*, III, 583–84, IV, 10; *TW*, II, 573.

2. *TW*, II, 572–73; council to Virginia Company, January 20, 1622/3, *RVCL*, IV, 10–11; Lurie, "Indian Cultural Adjustment," 48–50; Vaughan, "'Expulsion of the Salvages,'" 68–76; Fausz, "George Thorpe," 111–17.

Jamestown were awakened by a frantic settler named Richard Pace who had just rowed three miles from his farm across the river. Pace told his listeners—including the governor—that an Indian living in his house had warned him of a mass assault to be directed against the entire colony that very day. Convinced that this was more than just another false alarm, Wyatt prepared Jamestown for an attack and tried to alert nearby farms and settlements. But he was too late; the day of reckoning had begun.[3]

Just after sunrise Indians laden with food and furs appeared at English settlements all across Virginia, apparently conducting a common ritual of trading their goods for European wares. Some were met outside by the colonists, others were invited in to barter and perhaps share breakfast. Suddenly the visitors brandished hidden weapons or grabbed knives, chairs, pots, axes—whatever was at hand—and struck down everyone within reach. They spared neither "age or sexe, man, woman or childe; so sodaine in their cruell execution, that few or none discerned the weapon or blow that brought them to destruction." The surprise was nearly complete, and the slaughter was dreadful, for Opechancanough had planned to destroy all the English with a single overwhelming blow. Once the initial trap had been sprung, the warriors dashed from place to place, cutting down anyone they encountered on paths and byways, overrunning a house or hamlet, and then moving on to their next target. They were delayed a little by gruesome celebrations after each victory, "defacing, dragging, and mangling the dead carkasses into many pieces, and carrying some parts away in derision, and base and brutish triumph." Not everything went exactly according to plan in the hurry and confusion, and one isolated English family did not even learn of the attack until two days later.[4]

But few were so fortunate: more than three hundred settlers perished in the uprising. Though Pace's timely warning saved James-

3. Edward Waterhouse, *A Declaration of the State of the Colony and Affaires in Virginia* (London, 1622), *RVCL*, III, 555, 550–51. The most detailed account of the attack and the war that followed is Fausz, "Powhatan Uprising." The only other published account of the war is Powell, "Aftermath of the Massacre."

4. Waterhouse, *Declaration*, *RVCL*, III, 551, 555–56; Stith, *History of the First Discovery*, 213; *TW*, II, 576.

town and several other villages, the upriver settlements were practically swept away. The destruction would have been even greater had the Indians not shown an occasional lack of resolution. Despite their numerical advantage the natives avoided people and places that seemed prepared and failed to press their attack against determined resistance. The English were surprised to find that their assailants would "flye as so many Hares" from a man or woman carrying a musket, and a cornered Ralph Hamor single-handedly beat off a war party with only farm tools and brickbats. Nevertheless, Opechancanough had dealt the colony a devastating blow. On that "fatall Friday morning" his people had eliminated one-fourth or more of the English population and had reduced Virginia to chaos.[5]

In the aftermath of the massacre the English were stunned. One settler recalled that the fury of the attack "so dismaide the whole colony, as they allmost gave themselves for gone." For days the governor and the decimated council—four to six members had been slain—were so shocked and befuddled they were unable to decide upon a course of action. Another Virginian remembered that Wyatt seemed paralyzed while the natives "stood ripping open our gutts." As Indian raids continued and casualties mounted it became clear that the sprawling colony needed a more cohesive and defensible organization. Officials began "to re-collect the straglinge and woefull Inhabitants, so dismembered, into stronger bodies and more secure places." Most of the isolated farms and plantations which thus far had withstood the Indians were ordered abandoned and their residents consolidated into one of eight "great Bodies" along the James: Kecoughtan, Newport News, Jamestown, a cluster of plantations across the river, Jordan's Journey, and Shirley, Southampton and Flowerdew hundreds.[6]

An impromptu martial law was declared. Wyatt commissioned officers to oversee the withdrawals and command the eight strongholds. Each commander was to exercise "absolute power and Com-

5. Fausz, "Powhatan Uprising," 399; Waterhouse, *Declaration*, *RVCL*, III, 555–56; *TW*, II, 575–76.

6. "Discourse of the Old Company," *RVCL*, IV, 524; *TW*, II, 584; William Capps to John Ferrar, March 31, 1623, *RVCL*, IV, 76; council to Virginia Company, April, 1622, *ibid.*, III, 612–13; "A Briefe Declaration of the Plantation of Virginia duringe the first Twelve Years" [March, 1624], *JHB*, I, 37.

mand in all matters of warr," and the inhabitants were ordered "uppon paine of Death to obey him uppon all occacions, and to suffer themselves to be ordered and directed by him." Such extreme measures were necessary, Wyatt believed, because Virginia's very survival depended on his ability to maintain order and discipline among the angry, frightened people streaming into the strongholds. The governor's concern with order was well founded for the situation continued to deteriorate. The calamitous effect of the withdrawal proved to be even more damaging than the massacre. Food production—never one of early Virginia's strong points—was completely disrupted. In the necessary but perhaps overhasty evacuation large amounts of seed, food stores, and farm implements were left behind. Hundreds of laboriously cleared acres were abandoned. Military duties kept many men from engaging in spring planting, and the danger of Indian attacks further inhibited attempts at food production. Even the planting of corn posed an unexpected hazard. Settlers reported that the tall plants served as a perfect cover for the Indians, who "from tyme to tyme peeke out [pick off] many of our people whilst they are about theire weedinge and dressinge" in the cornfields.[7]

For a few months after the massacre some of the eight strongholds were in a virtual state of siege. "*The truth is*," wrote one settler, "*we dare scarce stepp out* of our dores." The upriver settlements probably suffered the most. The beleaguered inhabitants of Southampton urgently petitioned the governor for food because they were "infested" with hostile natives and were "not onlie putt from planting Corne, tobacco, and other nessarie Employmentes wherby they might be able to subsist, but also have no corne for the present to maintaine life." The dreadful shortage of food lasted for months, spawning despair and disease. "*We are all like to have the greatest famine in the land that ever was*," lamented a hungry settler. In desperation Wyatt commissioned officers to sail up the bay and collect food by whatever means necessary from any tribes they encountered. Its overcrowded strongholds ravaged by famine and disease, stung by Indian raids, and plagued by the continued influx of

7. Commission to Captain Roger Smith, April 13, 1622, *RVCL*, III, 609; council to Virginia Company, April, 1622, *ibid.*, 613–14; "Discourse of the Old Company," *ibid.*, IV, 525.

poorly provisioned immigrants, the reeling colony suffered appalling losses: hundreds died in the year following the massacre. Surveying the grisly chaos, treasurer George Sandys reported *"the lyveing being hardlie able to bury the dead."*[8] Once more Virginia tottered on the verge of collapse.

News of the massacre and abandonment of so many farms and villages came as a staggering blow to the Virginia Company in London. Everything that had been built over the years at a terrible cost in lives and money seemingly was being thrown away without a fight. Shocked, angry, demoralized, yet hopeful of somehow saving their investment in the New World, authorities in London made a fateful decision. A few years earlier company spokesmen had condemned "the stormes of raging cruelties" unleashed by the Spanish in Central America and had promised to treat the Virginia Indians "with faire and loving meanes, suiting to our English natures." Now such pacific gestures were forgotten. The massacre and the company's response to it marked a turning point in Anglo-Indian relations. Virginia was fighting for survival, and the instructions sent to Wyatt were brutally clear: "We must advise you to roote out from being any longer a people, so cursed a nation, ungratefull to all benefittes, and uncapable of all goodnesse: at least to the removeall of them so farr from you, as you may not only be out of danger, but out of feare of them, of whose faith and good meaning you can never be secure: wherefore as they have merited *let them have a perpetuall warre without peace or truce.*" To carry out this grim policy Wyatt was advised to adopt the tactics developed by John Smith and the military leaders—the feedfights—which had been so effective against the Indians' fragile subsistence economy.[9]

Besides initiating a policy of "perpetuall warre" against Ope-

8. Edward Hill to John Hill, April 14, 1623, *RVCL*, IV, 234; John Pountis' petition, June 15, 1622, *ibid.*, III, 652–53; Richard Frethorne to [?] Bateman, March 5, 1622/3, *ibid.*, IV, 41; Henry Brigg to Thomas Brigg [1623], *ibid.*, 236; commission to Captain Ralph Hamor, October 23, 1622, *ibid.*, III, 697; council to Virginia Company, January 20, 1622/3, *ibid.*, IV, 9–10; "Notes from Lists showing Total Number of Emigrants to Virginia" [1622], *ibid.*, III, 536–37; George Sandys to Samuel Wrote, March 28, 1623, *ibid.*, IV, 65.

9. Craven, *Dissolution of the Virginia Company*, 189–90, 198–202; [Robert Johnson], *Nova Britannia: Offering Most Excellent fruites by Planting in Virginia* (London, 1609), *Tracts*, I, 14; council to Virginia Company, April, 1622, *RVCL*, III, 614; Virginia Company to governor and council, August 1, 1622, *ibid.*, 671–72; Craven, "Indian Policy," 73–74.

chancanough (with whom only a year earlier the company had boasted of a "perpetuall league"), London ordered the immediate "replanting" of the lands recently abandoned to the Indians. Virginia officials were astounded. Wyatt complained that reversing the consolidation order would grievously weaken the colony and cause each settler to think only of himself. Sandys was more vehement: *"By yor Comaunding us to dispearse wee are like quicksilver throwne into the fire and hardlie to bee found in so vast a distance."* But desperation made the company adamant, and in time as the shock of the massacre wore off, growing numbers of colonists sought to escape the pestilential strongholds and return to their little farms. Throughout the fall and winter of 1622–1623 small groups of settlers cautiously slipped out of the fortifications and disappeared into the forests. Richard Pace, the savior of Jamestown, petitioned Wyatt to allow him to return home and "fortifie and strengthen the place with a good Company of able men." The governor granted Pace's request as well as hundreds of others from persons determined to prepare their abandoned fields for spring planting. In April, 1623, colonial authorities dutifully reported to the company that they had allowed "as many returne to theire Plantationes as have desired the same."[10]

As Wyatt and Sandys feared, these hardy souls faced a continuing threat. "Wee live in feare of the Enimy everie hower," wrote one settler a few miles below Jamestown, "for wee are in great danger, for our Plantation is very weake. . . . and the nighest helpe that Wee have is ten miles of us." And yet they carried on, adjusting to the rigors of life on the frontier. Day-to-day existence was a gamble. Three years after the massacre a settler wrote that when "wee goe out in the morning, wee know not whether wee shall ever returne; working with our Hoe in one hand, and our Peece or Sword in the other, etc." Violent death was common. "Whilest I was a writing these lines," one farmer calmly noted in a letter to

10. Virginia Company to governor and council, August 1, 1622, *RVCL*, III, 670; council to Virginia Company, January 20, 1622/3, *ibid.*, IV, 12; Sandys to Wrote, March 28, 1623, and Sandys to Sir Samuel Sandys, March 30, 1623, *ibid.*, 66, 73; Richard Pace's petition [1622], *ibid.*, III, 682; council to Virginia Company, April 4, 1623, *ibid.*, IV, 99.

his parents in England, "newes was brought me of the killing of one, and the carrying away prisoner of another of my neighbours, by the Indians . . . and but two daies agoe there was another that had his braines beaten out by the Indians, in the next Plantation to us." Other letters to the homeland were filled with similar stories.[11]

Despite their losses most of the farmers hung on, buoyed up by the recent distribution of the colony's supply of weapons. In the aftermath of the massacre it seemed clear that firearms were the only possible means of defending replanted farmsteads. Everyone knew the Indians were wary of guns. They were startled by loud reports and occasionally ran away merely at the sight of a musket.[12] But to defend every house and hamlet in the colony would require placing guns and other weapons permanently in the hands of hundreds or thousands of unsupervised individuals—an alarming innovation for the seventeenth century. Up to this time relatively few Virginians possessed their own weapons, and the supply of arms left over from the military regime was kept locked away in company magazines scattered about the colony. The Indian threat was so great and so immediate, however, that provincial authorities apparently decided to arm the population in the hope of dramatically improving the overall defensive posture of the colony. Perhaps no other event of the period so plainly reveals the desperate plight of the Virginia colony.

Wyatt soon discovered there were not enough weapons in the colony to go around. He informed London that nearly half of his able-bodied men were "utterly unprovided" with arms or armor. The governor asked that a large supply of weapons be sent at once and that future immigrants carry their own weapons with them. Upon receiving this alarming news company officials convinced King James to dispatch to Virginia a collection of obsolescent weapons stored in the Tower of London. The lot included "1000 browne bills, 400 bowes, and bowestaves, 800 shefs of Arrowes, 700 Callivers, 300 short pistolls with fire lockes, and 300 harquibussies

11. Richard Frethorne to his parents, March 20, April 3, 1623, *ibid.*, IV, 58–60; Purchas, *Hakluytus Posthumus*, XIX, 210–11.

12. Waterhouse, *Declaration*, *RVCL*, III, 555; Morgan, *American Slavery*, 108–30.

. . . 2000 skulls of Iron, 100 brigandines, 40 plate Coates and 400 shirtes, and Coates of Maile." These weapons, particularly the thirteen hundred firearms, were considered "unfitt for any moderne service" in England or Europe, but it was hoped they would be more than adequate against the Indians. (The longbows and arrows eventually were sent to Bermuda rather than Virginia. Officials feared the Indians might capture some of these weapons and turn them against the colonists.)[13]

The shipment of Tower arms and assorted smaller parcels of weapons arrived at Jamestown in late 1622 at about the time the replanting got under way. As they had done in the past, London officials specified that these company-owned weapons should "be kept in a Common Store or Armory in Virginia for the Generall service of the whole Colony upon all occasions." But provincial authorities quietly ignored these instructions and distributed the weapons to those who needed them, just as had been done with the company weapons already in Virginia. An inventory of military stores at Jamestown less than two years later listed a few old cannons and some rusty armor but did not mention firearms and other personal weapons except to note that such equipment was "dispersed in the Cunttrie." Indeed, by 1624 there apparently no longer was an official "munition house" at Jamestown or anywhere else in the colony.[14] This quiet but revolutionary dispersal of arms made possible much of what happened later in Virginia's struggle for survival against the natives. It also initiated a troublesome and dangerous American tradition.

While these events unfolded, the English settlers went on the offensive with a vengeance. By the summer of 1622 Indian attacks against the strongholds had fallen off, giving the colonists an opportunity to strike back if they could muster sufficient strength to

13. Council to Virginia Company, April, 1622, *RVCL*, III, 614; warrant to the lord treasurer, September, 1622, *ibid.*, 676; Virginia Company minutes, August 14, November 20, 1622, *ibid.*, II, 100, 135. Calivers and harquebusses were firearms somewhat lighter than muskets. Brigandines were vests of metal plates covered with leather or canvas.

14. Virginia Company minutes, August 14, 1622, *ibid.*, II, 100; Jester and Hiden, *Adventurers of Purse and Person*, 27; John Harvey, "A Briefe Declaration of the State of Virginia at my Comminge from Thence in February 1624," *Collections*, 73.

do so. Wyatt was determined to try. In rousing proclamations he reminded his fellow Virginians of "those vexed Soules and troubled Spirites of ours, when in this last outrage of these Infidelles we were forced to stand and gaze at our distressed bretheren, fryinge in the furie of our enimies, and could not relieve them." The survivors, he said, must use "shuch force and meanes, as God at present doth aford unto us . . . to reveng their cruell deedes." These were brave words indeed from the leader of a band of unruly, demoralized men so few in number that for a time Wyatt and his councillors had to stand watch along the palisades at Jamestown.[15] The translation of these words into action is impressive.

During the summer and early fall of 1622 the colonists repeatedly lashed out at their antagonists. Wyatt commissioned officers to sally forth and "make warr, kill, spoile, and take by force" anything of value to the enemy. Former governor Yeardley, an old soldier and Wyatt's principal lieutenant, led an expedition of three hundred men against the Nansemonds, Pamunkeys, and other tribes. This large force—which must have included nearly every armed man in Virginia—sailed downriver from Jamestown to the village of the Nansemonds to begin what became a familiar pattern. The Indians refused to fight, burned or abandoned their houses, and fled with whatever they could carry, so that the frustrated English "did make no slaughter amongst them for revenge." A little later at Opechancanough's village of Pamunkey (near present-day West Point), the natives carried off much of their corn while a small party pretended to parley with Yeardley on the banks of the river. After a time the colonists realized they were being tricked, brushed aside the remaining natives, destroyed the town, and seized what food and booty they could find. At least seven other raids were carried out against tribes all across tidewater Virginia. Captains William Powell and Nathaniel Butler with eighty men razed Chickahominy villages upriver from Jamestown, the Indians as usual "not daring to resist them." Captain John West's raiders fell upon the Tanx Powhatans and Captain Sandys' troops attacked the Tap-

15. Earle, "Environment, Disease, and Mortality," 107; commissions to Yeardley, June 20, September 10, 1622, *RVCL*, III, 656, 678–89; Sandys to Wrote, March 28, 1623, *ibid.*, IV, 66.

pahannocks with much the same results. Captains Isaac Madison and Ralph Hamor (who had demonstrated his mettle during the massacre) journeyed to the Potomac River, where their men destroyed several villages. A bit south of there Captain William Tucker's force sought out the Rappahannocks "to take revenge uppon them, as Confederates with Apochankeno."[16]

"Wee have anticipated your desires by settinge uppon the Indyans in all places," the council declared to London in January, 1623. The operations were orgies of destruction, and in that sense they were successful, but surprisingly little blood was shed: perhaps a dozen Indians were killed and a handful of colonists were killed and wounded. Losses on both sides were low because the natives ran away from English raiding parties and the heavily encumbered settlers were unable to pursue them. It quickly became apparent to colonial authorities once more that the Indians were "an enemy nott suddenlie to be destroyde with the sworde by reasone of theire swyftnes of foote, and advantages of the woodes, to which uppon all our assaultes they retyre." And yet, despite the absence of any major battles, the Indians suffered badly from the long-range effects of these raids. During the following winter hundreds fell victim to exposure, starvation, and disease. Authorities in Jamestown estimated that more natives died over the winter than "hath been slayne before since the begininge of the Colonie." Unfortunately, the colonists suffered heavy losses of their own during these same months from similar causes. The ship that brought the king's gift of Tower arms in December also carried a devastating pestilence. "Extreame hath beene the mortalitie of this yeare," wrote Sandys, "which I am afraid hath dobled the Nomber of those which were massacred." But, he noted, Virginia's "small and sicklie forces" had driven the natives back into the wilderness.[17] Grim as the situation was, the English were gaining the upper hand.

With the spring came a jarring setback. In April, 1623, Captain

16. Commission to Yeardley, September 10, 1622, *RVCL*, III, 67–69; council to Virginia Company, January 20, 1622/3, *ibid.*, IV, 9; *TW*, II, 590–603; "Good Newes from Virginia," 351–58.

17. Council to Virginia Company, January 20, 1622/3, *RVCL*, IV, 9–10; George Sandys to Sir Miles Sandys and John Ferrar, March 30, 1623, *ibid.*, 25, 71; *TW*, II, 594, 600.

Henry Spelman and some twenty men were wiped out on the banks of the Potomac River. Why Spelman fell victim to the Indians is difficult to understand. He was "a warie man well acquainted" with Indian treachery; as a boy living with Powhatan he had witnessed the ambush and destruction of a large group of colonists in 1609. Nevertheless, when he and his men arrived at a Pascoticon village to trade for corn, they walked into an ambush and were overwhelmed and killed immediately. The Pascoticons then set out in their canoes to seize the merchantman *Tyger* riding in midstream, her skeleton crew awaiting Spelman's return. By a stroke of luck or quick thinking one of the sailors manning the *Tyger* touched off a cannon which so frightened the Indians scrambling aboard that they jumped into the river. Granted this brief reprieve, the crew "whiffed up sayles" and made their way back to Jamestown. The colonists were shocked at this unexpected defeat. Besides the loss of experienced men (Spelman ironically was the colony's premier interpreter and Indian expert), a substantial quantity of weapons and trade goods had fallen into the hands of the Indians. Even more ominous was the attack on the *Tyger*, for the natives had never before attempted to take a full-size ship.[18]

Shortly after this incident, and perhaps partly in reaction to it, the Virginians carried out a treacherous gambit of their own. Early in 1623 two Indians captured in a skirmish divulged that several Englishwomen were being held captive by Opechancanough. While the colonists were attempting to negotiate the release of these prisoners, Opechancanough unexpectedly asked for a cessation of hostilities and a general prisoner exchange. The Virginians must have been pleased to hear the chief's messenger admit that "many of his People were starved, by our takinge Away theire Corne and burninge theire howses" and that the Indians only wished to live in peace and rebuild their ruined towns. The governor agreed to an armistice, ostensibly to secure the return of the prisoners.[19]

Now it was Opechancanough's turn to be fooled. Wyatt's accept-

18. Peter Arundel to William Canning, April, 1623, *RVCL*, IV, 89; Frethorne to his parents, March 20, 1623, *ibid.*, 61.

19. Council to Virginia Company, April 4, 1623, *ibid.*, IV, 98–99; Brown, *First Republic in America*, 507, 511–12.

ance of the Indian offer was a ruse intended to lure the elusive enemy within striking distance. As the governor had hoped, the cease-fire encouraged the natives to return to their old villages and replant their wasted cornfields. Authorities noted the strength and location of the various tribes and bided their time until it was too late in the season for the natives to plant a new food crop. Some settlers did not understand or appreciate such subtle strategy and chafed at the delay. "Swoondes," one raged, "I Could Tear myselfe to see what weatherbeaten Crowes wee are, to suffer the Heathen kennell of dogges to indent with us in this order." The truce came to an end in May, 1623, when Wyatt dispatched Captain William Tucker and twelve volunteers to sail up the York River "neere to the seate of Appochankano" and there pick up the English prisoners. Tucker waited aboard ship until the natives had delivered the captive women. He and his men then went ashore to parley, armed to the teeth and carrying several butts of poisoned wine. After a good deal of discussion and "manye fayned speches" of friendship, Tucker proposed a toast to the assembled Indian leaders. They agreed and joined him in gulping down the wine. They did not notice, however, that Tucker's wine came from a separate container. Moments later the poison began to take effect and Tucker ordered his little band to fire "a volie of shotte" into the stricken assemblage. After quickly surveying the carnage and estimating that about two hundred Indians had been killed, the English scrambled back aboard their shallops and set off for Jamestown. As they sailed down the York they managed to kill another fifty or so Indians and brought along "parte of their heades" as souvenirs. The colonists at first thought Opechancanough was among the dead at Pamunkey, "it beinge impossable, that he should escape, the designe beinge Chieflie uppon his persone," but the wily leader somehow had survived the poison and evaded the bullets. Nevertheless, there was good news for a change at Jamestown, and Robert Bennett expressed a common sentiment when he told his brother that this episode "wilbe a great desmayinge to the blodye infidelles."[20]

20. Council to Virginia Company, April 4, 1623, *RVCL*, IV, 99; William Capps to Thomas Winston [March or April, 1623], *ibid.*, 37–38; commission to Captain William Tucker, May 12, 1623, *ibid.*, 190; Robert Bennett to Edward Bennett, June 9, 1623, *ibid.*, 221; council to Virginia Company [May or June, 1623], *ibid.*, 102.

Authorities in England took a somewhat dimmer view of the affair. Wyatt informed his superiors of what had happened and predicted that since it was now too late for the Indians to retire into the woods and plant another corn crop, the colonists would "geve them shortly a blow, That shall neere or altogether Ruinate them." The upright gentlemen who administered the Virginia Company did not entirely approve of making war by such dishonorable means, even against treacherous savages, and they so informed Jamestown. The Virginians returned a bristling if somewhat confusing answer: "Wheras we are advised by you to observe rules of Justice with these barberous and perfidious enemys, *wee hold nothinge injuste, that may tend to theire ruine,* (except breach of faith)[.] Stratagems were ever allowed against all enemies, *but with these neither fayre Warr nor good quarter is ever to be held,* nor is there other hope of theire subversione, who ever may informe you to the Contrarie." The massacre, the Spelman ambush, the killing of male prisoners, and like incidents had confirmed the colonists' belief that the natives were treacherous, cowardly, barbarous, and implacably hostile. The Indians had behaved like animals. Henceforth they would be treated as such. Any tactics that might help to exterminate this savage vermin now were acceptable to the colonists.[21]

As Wyatt had hoped, the summer of 1623 was a time of unrelieved calamity for the Indians. Opechancanough and his people were tied to their defenseless cornfields and could only await the inevitable. In July and August six groups of Virginians sallied forth under Wyatt's stern orders "to pursue the Salvages with fire and Sword" and destroy their food and shelter. "God sende us vyctrie," prayed one settler-soldier on the eve of the offensive, for "we macke noe question god asistinge." His prayers were answered when Captain William Pierce's men pushed upriver to chastise the Chickahominies while Captain Samuel Mathews and his troops struck the Tanx Powhatans' village near the falls of the James. Captain Nathaniel West raided the towns of the Appomattocks and Tanx Weyanokes, and the redoubtable William Tucker attacked the Nan-

21. Council to Virginia Company, April 4, 1623, and January 30, 1623/4, *ibid.*, IV, 102, 451; Craven, "Indian Policy," 73; Vaughan, "'Expulsion of the Salvages,'" 77–79; Nash, "Image of the Indian," 217–20.

semonds and Wariscoyacks on the south side of the James. A week later Tucker paid a second call on the Nansemonds and Captain Isaac Madison marched against the Great Weyanokes. These combined attacks dealt the main tribes along the James River a heavy blow.[22]

In November the English struck again. Wyatt had planned to attack earlier, but he waited to give his people enough time to harvest their crops. This delay allowed the Indians to gather and hide what was left of their corn, so the settlers aimed at locating and destroying enemy stockpiles of food. Warrants and commissions were issued, men assembled, and another series of raids began, this time to the north. Wyatt led about one hundred men to the Potomac River "to revenge the trecherie of the Pascoticons" for the Spelman ambush. There the raiders "putt many to the swoorde" and destroyed the native towns along with a "marvelous quantetie of Corne" which had been hidden in the woods nearby. To follow up this victory the governor planned to use the neighboring Patawomeke or Potomac tribe, "ancyent alies" of the English, as guides in an attack on the Pamunkeys, but he was unable to do so before winter brought an end to active campaigning. The first phase of the war was over.[23]

22. Commissions to Captain William Pierce and others, July 17, 23, 1623, *RVCL*, IV, 250–51; Bennett to Bennett, June 9, 1623, *ibid.*, 222; council to Virginia Company, January 30, 1623/4, *ibid.*, 450.

23. Warrants to Captain Isaac Madison and others, October 20, 1623, *ibid.*, 292; council to Virginia Company, January 30, 1623/4, *ibid.*, 450–51.

3. Emergence of the Militia

By 1624 Virginia no longer was in danger of extinction. The epidemic was abating, food production was increasing, and everywhere the Indians were on the defensive. There was, however, one nagging problem. The demise of the military regime left Virginia without any institutionalized means of organizing and supporting military operations. The current method of carrying on the war amounted to little more than rounding up a suitable number of colonists and setting off after the Indians. It was amateurish, arbitrary, erratic, and, above all, unpopular. By the end of the second summer of the war public dissatisfaction with the military system—or the lack thereof—was becoming serious.[1]

When Wyatt unleashed the settlers' initial counterattack in 1622 he instructed Yeardley to collect such men *"as he shall find willing"* to go on the expedition. John Smith claimed that Yeardley was able to recruit only those who "would leave their private businesse." Smith's criticism was premature, for at that time the settlers "could not freely imploy themselves in plantinge" because they had withdrawn into the strongholds. Very few colonists had any "private businesse" in the six or eight months following the massacre. The strongholds were overcrowded, unhealthy, and short of food and the settlers were eager for revenge, so Yeardley had no trouble assembling about three hundred volunteers.[2]

The settlers' feelings had changed over the winter of 1622–1623 when they dispersed to reoccupy and rebuild their little farms. Some people now thought operations against the Indians should be handled by someone other than themselves. Wyatt noted that many settlers "having done and suffered much here thinke themselves Emeritos milites and free from publique dutyes." The number of volunteers dropped, and the governor had to authorize Captain William Pierce

1. The only recorded instance of outright refusal to serve is the case of one Richard Bickley, who declined "to take armes and discharge his publick dutye." He was "layed neck and heeles 12 howers" and fined (May 7, 1627, *Minutes*, 148).

2. Commission to Yeardley, September 10, 1622, *RVCL*, III, 67–68; *TW*, II, 599; "Discourse of the Old Company," *RVCL*, IV, 519–21.

"to choose" from the Jamestown area "such and so many as he in his discretion shall think fittest for service." All officers were directed to support Pierce in this task in case any colonists declined to participate in "so generall and necessarie a service." Moreover, to uphold "the discipline of warr," Pierce and other officers were granted the power to inflict all punishments short of death on their troops. In October, 1623, Captain Isaac Madison was similarly authorized *"to leavy* (with as much equalitie and indiferencie as he may) through all the Plantations from Flowerdieu Hundred uppward fouretie able and sufficient men." Residents of this area were cautioned "to yeeld ready abedience" or "answer the contrary at theire uttermost perill."[3] Such impressments and stern warnings indicate a distinct decline in martial enthusiasm among the colonists by 1623.

The problem was primarily economic. "The Chiefe tyme of doeinge the emynie most spoyle" was the very time the settlers could least afford to be away from their farms. Virginians pressed for military duty between spring and fall complained that when "a man be taken from his private labour but for a day or two it turnes to his great prejudice" because "he hath no meanes to susteyne himselfe but what he getts by his owne industrie." Governor Wyatt must have recognized the legitimacy of such complaints because he tried to schedule military operations at the least disruptive times.[4]

Nevertheless, the war could not be fought in fits and starts dictated by popular demand, and the assembly that met in March, 1624, spent much time reviewing the military situation. The legislators agreed to continue the feedfights and resolved that in July "the Inhabitants of every Corporatione shall falle uppon theire adjoyninge Salvages" with as much force as possible. Having settled on tactics and timetables, the legislators then attempted to make military service less onerous and capricious. Those "olde planters"

3. Wyatt to his father, April 4, 1623, *RVCL*, IV, 237; commissions to Captain William Pierce and others, July 17, 23, 1623, *ibid.*, 250–51; warrants to Captain Isaac Madison and others, October 20, 1623, *ibid.*, 292.

4. Council to Virginia Company, January 30, 1623/4, *ibid.*, 450–51; "Notes for an Answer to the Propositions made by Lord Chichester" [August or September, 1623], *ibid.*, 260–61; Morgan, *American Slavery*, 178; Breen, "Looking Out for Number One," 342–57.

who had arrived in Virginia before 1612 no longer were subject to active military service. Those who did serve might be comforted by the knowledge that now an injured or wounded soldier would be cared for at public expense, and a maimed or crippled soldier would be maintained permanently at public expense "accordinge to his persone and qualitie." Most important, a method of compensation was established to reduce substantially the economic hardship inflicted on those individuals pressed for service. The lawmakers decided that "such persons as remaine at home, shall ratably bere out the labours of such as are abroad upon the march, by giveinge [so many] dayes workes in their ground untill their returne." Area commanders were ordered to see that the compensatory labor was assigned "equally by just computation and with all indifferently, and see it duely executed."[5]

Henceforth, when a man was called upon to serve in a military capacity, he could do so knowing that his farm and family were being cared for under the stern eye of the local commander. Public service no longer was a penalty. Men now had a legal obligation not only to defend themselves and the colony but also to provide for one another in times of crisis. It probably is not inaccurate to say that the Virginia militia was established in a very rudimentary form by the general assembly of 1624. And although the militia would not develop into a mature institution for many years, even in its infancy it differed from its contemporary English counterpart in that it was a combat organization composed of nearly every adult male in the colony.

The new system was immediately put to the test. Taking up where he had left off the previous fall, Wyatt led a small force up the York to do battle with Opechancanough at Pamunkey. To everyone's surprise the Indians stood and fought. The result was the only pitched battle of the war. Fighting raged for two July days through woods and fields around the native town. The Pamunkeys recently had made "greate braggs" to other tribes about how they would rout the English. Now they struggled furiously to make good their

5. Orders, March 5, 1623/4, *RVCL*, IV, 580–84; July 12, 1624, *Minutes*, 18; Shea, "First American Militia," 16.

boasts. Wyatt and his sixty heavily armored "Fyghtinge men" were hard-pressed to withstand attack after attack by hundreds of young warriors literally driven into battle by club-swinging elders. Sixteen Englishmen were wounded but none were killed and the troops held firm. Indian casualties mounted with each repulse. By the end of the second day the exhausted natives "were so discoraged, that they gave over fightinge and dismayedly, stood most ruthfully [ruefully] lookinge one while theire Corne was Cutt downe." The troops then departed to spread the word of their victory. Wyatt intended to follow up this success with raids along the Mattaponi River, but the lengthy clash at Pamunkey seriously depleted Virginia's supply of gunpowder and caused him to suspend further offensive operations.[6]

The year 1624 probably was the turning point of the war. While Indian strength declined Virginia was slowly recovering from the recent string of catastrophes. This year "the Colony hath very well stoode to health," wrote the council, for "God hath sent us a plentifull harvest of Corne and the industrious are well stored with other provisiones, soe that exceptinge the number of men the Colony hath worne owt the Skarrs of the massacre."[7]

The year 1624 also was the end of the line for the Virginia Company. King James finally dissolved the bankrupt, faction-ridden organization and brought the colony under direct royal supervision. This event was of great future significance as the beginning of what would become the British Empire, but it had little immediate impact on Virginia. Wyatt and the councillors retained their positions, and the provincial government continued to operate under the 1619 charter, though now in the name of the king. The crown sent a number of commissioners to the colony at this time to ascertain the true condition of the new royal property. Not surprisingly, defense was one of the focal points of their investigation.[8]

The commissioners met with the leaders of the colony and re-

6. Council to Earl of Southampton and Virginia Company, December 2, 1624, *RVCL*, IV, 507–508.

7. *Ibid.*

8. Craven, *Dissolution of the Virginia Company*, 318–22; Virginia Company to governor and council, August 26, 1624, *RVCL*, IV, 501–504; governor and council to Privy Council, April 6, 1626, *ibid.*, 572.

ceived an analysis of the problems of irregular warfare. It was difficult even with firearms to defend so many scattered fixed points, authorities acknowledged, for the natives shrewdly relied on "ambushes and suddein incursions where they see their advantages." There was no doubt the colonists had gained the upper hand in recent months, but they were unable to deliver a knockout blow against so elusive an enemy. Consequently, there was little chance of an early end to the fighting. The greatest problem at this point was the need for constant vigilance. Uncertainty about the Indians' whereabouts and intentions forced people to watch and ward "as if the enymie weare at all tymes present," prevented them from allowing their cattle to forage freely in the woods, and kept them from hunting and fishing to supplement their diet.[9]

The commissioners were impressed by the severity of the situation and drew up four suggestions to be placed before the king and Privy Council for the better defense of the embattled royal colony. First, thinly settled areas should be strengthened with "newe Commers" from England. Second, a palisade should be constructed across the peninsula between the James and the York. Third, the settlers should be drilled regularly in the military arts and a supply of arms and ammunition should be made available to the colony. Fourth, a permanent force of two hundred men should be created "to infest the Indians" day and night. Their task completed, the commissioners returned to England.[10] All but the last of their four suggestions would be implemented to some degree over the next few years, particularly during commissioner Sir John Harvey's term as governor, but for the moment the new royal colony of Virginia carried on as usual.

Upon learning of the death of his father, Francis Wyatt followed the commissioners home, his service in Virginia temporarily at an end. In his place the king appointed George Yeardley. The old soldier and former governor took command once again just as Virginia entered a prolonged period of military inactivity. The shortage of gunpowder that developed in 1624 forced the colonists to forego

9. "The Generall Assemblies Replie," March 2, 1623/4, *JHB*, I, 38; Harvey, "Briefe Declaration," *Collections*, 70–71.

10. Harvey, "Briefe Declaration," *Collections*, 69–70, 72–73.

their regular seasonal attacks against the Indians in 1625 and 1626 and hampered military operations for the rest of the war.[11]

During this period of inactivity provincial authorities continued to wrestle with the problem of security. Further adjustments and refinements were made in the composition of the militia. New arrivals, however welcome, were often sickly after their long voyage and were totally unprepared for the wilderness and therefore were absolved temporarily from military service. They were of little use until they became healthier and more experienced, a process the veterans called "seasoning." In the past a shortage of men had forced the governor to use even the greenest settlers as soldiers; now that no longer was necessary. Newcomers henceforth were free from military duty and taxes their first year in Virginia but were, of course, expected to defend their places of residence against enemy attack. All other males from seventeen—later sixteen—to sixty except the "olde planters" were eligible for military duty and would be taxed for "maintenance of the Warrs proportionably to their abilities." Authorities were careful to add that officers and gentlemen would not be forced to serve as common soldiers "or in places Inferior to their degrees, unless in cases of extream necessity."[12]

Defensive measures were intensified. Palisades were ordered erected around individual houses. Men were instructed to attend church with their arms "fixed and in good order" to prevent sabbath ambushes. Local commanders were required to call their people together at regular intervals to "exercyse and drill them, wherby they may be made the more fitt for service uppon any occasione." (This seems to have been the first training statute issued since the military regime and apparently resulted from the commissioners' visit.) Everyone was reminded to "carefully stand uppon their guard, keepe sentinell uppon their workemen by day, and keepe good watch by night, shutting and makeing fast the gates of their forts, not suffering any single man to stragle abroad, whereby all daunger may

11. Commission to Yeardley, September 15, 1624, *RVCL*, IV, 504; governor and council to commissioners, January 4, 1625/6, *ibid.*, 568–69; Harvey, "Briefe Declaration," *Collections*, 61–62.

12. Instructions to Yeardley, April 19, 1626, CO 5/1354, ff. 262–69; August 7, 8, 1626, *Minutes*, 104–107.

be prevented." Settlers who violated these rules were penalized. William Barnes and Robert Paramore of Jamestown were caught napping while on watch and spent the next three days clearing away underbrush from the walls of the town.[13]

These measures were a prelude to another round of fighting. The Indians had remained quiet during the lull and were reported to be "infinitly desirous" of peace, but Yeardley was not so inclined. He slowly accumulated a modest stockpile of powder as the natives again dribbled back to their old towns. In August, 1627, the Virginians unexpectedly launched a major offensive against the tidewater tribes and their ripening corn crop. A decoy was used to ensure a more complete surprise. The merchantman *Virgin* sailed up the York toward Pamunkey to threaten Opechancanough while the real blows fell further south. The attacks followed the usual pattern. Troops from each area assembled at the larger villages and sailed to strike their assigned targets: the Tanx Powhatan, Weyanoke, Appomattock, Nansemond, Chickahominy, Tappahannock, Wariscoyack, and Chesapeake tribes. In October a combined force assaulted the Pamunkeys. The English again wrecked the flimsy native towns and destroyed large quantities of corn. This campaign was Yeardley's last hurrah; he died in November. Captain Francis West claimed that had the settlers not been "disabled by a Common Scarsitye of Shott" during the offensive they would have achieved the "utter ruine and extirpation" of the entire Powhatan confederation.[14]

The Indians fought back as best they could by sniping at stragglers and isolated farms. One of their victims was John Throgmoton, who was working in a field "nere unto the woods" one fall morning when he was "wounded and shott in the body." He died a short time later. The Indians also managed to carry four colonists off to Pamunkey. As they had done in 1623, authorities in Jamestown decided to ransom the captives by agreeing to Opechancanough's demands for an end to the fighting. A treaty was drawn up

13. April 3, June 25, 1627, August 7, 8, July 28, 1626, *Minutes*, 147, 104–107, 150.
14. Governor and council to commissioners, January 4, 1625/6, *RVCL*, IV, 569; July 4, 1627, *Minutes*, 151; governor and council to Privy Council, December 20, 1627, CO 1/4, f. 88.

in which the natives promised to stay away from English settlements and livestock. The council warned the settlers that this treaty was nothing more than a convenient means of recovering the captives; it would be dissolved at the first opportunity. The shaky cease-fire lasted about six months, during which time the captives were released and Yeardley's successor, Sir John Harvey, was appointed.[15]

The cessation of hostilities had a strange effect on the settlers. Despite repeated warnings from their leaders to remain alert during the armistice, many of the English turned their full attention to the cultivation of tobacco. Within a few months they had grown so complacent they "utterly neglected eyther to stand uppon their guard or to keepe their Arms fitt and ready about them." Such aberrant behavior may have been caused by the boom in tobacco prices in the second half of the decade. But whatever the reason, this relaxed state was intolerable, particularly because the Indians tended to ignore the treaty provisions. The only way to prevent a second massacre from eventually occurring seemed to be to "proclayme and maintayne enmity and warres with all the Indians of these partes." At the end of January, 1629, the council decided that for the good of the colony the current agreement with the natives should be "utterlye extincte and dissanulled." Virginia was better off at war than at peace. An Indian was captured and then released to notify Opechancanough that the treaty was being abrogated—a curiously civil touch in a barbarous war.[16]

A peaceful spring followed, as though both sides were reluctant to renew the fighting. The Indians ran off cattle and swine and generally made a nuisance of themselves but did little real damage. Then in midsummer a party of five settlers was ambushed and wiped out. Enraged at this enemy success—the last Indian victory of the war—colonial troops once again marched out to raze towns and crops. Later in the year the natives received an even more devastating blow. An Indian warrior defected to the English and led a

15. September 17, 1627, April 24, August 12, 1628, *Minutes*, 153, 172, 484; instructions to Harvey, August 6, 1628, *Acts of the Privy Council*, 127–28.

16. January 31, March 4, 1628/9, *Minutes*, 184–85, 189–90, 198; Menard, "Note on Chesapeake Tobacco Prices," 401–10; Morgan, "First American Boom," 177.

raiding party to hidden cornfields, where the settlers "wrought more spoil and revenge than they had done since the great massacre."[17]

By now the scales had tipped overwhelmingly in favor of the settlers. William Pierce estimated that Virginia could muster more than two thousand able-bodied men for military service, a far cry from the little bands of hungry farmers staggering out to do battle in 1622. Lack of ammunition was a chronic problem, but there was as yet no noticeable shortage of weapons. John Smith noted approvingly from London that most settlers possessed "a Peece, a Jacke, a Coat of Maile, a Sword, or Rapier; and everie Holy-day, everie Plantation doth exercise their men in Armes, by which meanes . . . the most part of them are most excellent markmen." The crown now not only approved of this martial spirit (as long as it was limited to the colonies) but insisted that in the future every settler provide himself with arms, armor, and ammunition.[18]

Late in the year the assembly met and added the final wartime touches to the emerging militia system. The colony was divided into four military districts. Three of these districts were to launch coordinated attacks against their neighboring Indians in March, July, and November of every year. Persons living on either side of the James River above Flowerdew Hundred were expected to do "all manner of spoile and offence to the Indians that may possibly bee effected." Those living between Flowerdew and Hog Island were to do the same, as were the people in the third and smallest district around Wariscoyack on the south side. Residents of the fourth district, which included the lower peninsula and the Eastern Shore, were ordered to strike the Pamunkeys and Nansemonds every summer and fall. The command structure was modified to allow quicker response and greater flexibility. Local commanders were authorized to raise troops whenever "they in their discretion shall deeme it convenient to cleare the woods and the parts neere adjoyning when the Indians shall bee a hunting or when they have

17. July, 1629, *Minutes*, 198, 484; Joseph Mead to Sir Martin Stuteville, January 23, 1629/30, in Birch, *Court and Times of Charles the First*, II, 53–54.

18. William Pierce, "A relation in generall of the present state of his Majesties Colony in Virginia" [1629], CO 1/5, ff. 69–70; *TW*, II, 886.

any certaine knowledge of the Indian's aboad in those places."[19] By the end of 1629 the Virginians finally had a workable military structure: manpower, weapons, organization, training, strategy, and tactics.

The conflict dragged on into the 1630s, but it no longer was much of a contest. The natives made only feeble efforts to harass the colonists, who hammered away at them with monotonous regularity. The legislators annually declared the Indians to be their "irreconcileable enemyes" and brushed aside Opechancanough's peace overtures. In 1631 the English began a project that would greatly increase their strength and security. For years they had talked of building a wall across the narrow waist of the peninsula between the James and the York. Similar smaller barriers once had secured Henrico and other settlements along the upper James from Indian attack; perhaps the same could be done on a larger scale. Wyatt was the main proponent of this scheme and called it "a worke of more consequence, then discovery of Mines, the South Sea, or what project soever." He suggested it to the royal commissioners, and in 1626 he contracted with two entrepreneurs to build the wall for £1,200 in "readie money" plus £100 annually for upkeep. But in spite of Commissioner Harvey's enthusiastic support the crown refused to provide the funds, and the project languished. Wyatt's sudden departure and Yeardley's death prevented any further action for several years.[20]

When Harvey became governor he convinced the assembly to finance construction of the wall at once through land grants rather than continue waiting for royal handouts. The project was carried out in two stages. A small fortified settlement was established at Chiskiack, where Queen's Creek flows into the York (a short distance above the present Yorktown). This outpost was to be the northern terminus of the wall and would also serve as an advanced base of operations against the Pamunkey towns some twenty miles to the northwest. Next a labor battalion was raised in much the

19. October 16, 1629, *JHB*, I, 52–53.

20. September 4, 1632, *Statutes*, I, 199; Harvey to Viscount Dorchester, April 15, 1630, CO 1/5, f. 176; governor and council to Privy Council, May 17, 1626, CO 1/4, ff. 21–23; Harvey, "Briefe Declaration," *Collections*, 72–73.

same manner as a militia force and sent to Middle Plantation (now Williamsburg), a tiny hamlet on a low ridge midway between the two rivers. There the men began to cut a swath through the forest and erect the wall. When finally completed in the spring of 1633, the wall ran south from the head of Queen's Creek through Middle Plantation to the head of College or Archer's Hope Creek, a distance of about six miles. The wall was a simple palisade of upright logs reinforced every few hundred feet by blockhouses "within Comaund of Muskett Shott one of another." Persons who settled along the path of the wall received title to a blockhouse and fifty acres of land. They served as a permanent garrison and maintenance force. It was a massive project for its time, and Harvey was justly proud of it. The palisade, he reported to London, had "secured a great part of the Countrey from the incursions of the natives" and given the settlers "a safe range for their Cattle neere as bigg as Kent."[21]

The First Tidewater War sputtered to a close just about the time the wall was completed and manned. Why the war ended when it did is difficult to discern; details about this period are scarce. All we know is that sometime in late 1632 a truce was worked out with the Powhatan confederation and the Chickahominies. The terms are unknown, though presumably both sides agreed to have as little to do with one another as possible. Thus the war ended somewhat inconclusively. The following year Harvey observed that as yet the English remained "upon good termes with the Indian, but stand at all tymes upon our guarde." As the months passed without a serious outbreak of fighting, life slowly returned to normal.[22]

Virginia had changed during the war. The commercial enterprise staffed by transient laborers had become a largely self-governing royal colony with a permanent population and a viable economic system based on tobacco cultivation. Toward the end of the war

21. Harvey to Viscount Dorchester, May 29, 1630, CO 1/5, f. 195; October 8, 1630, *Minutes*, 479; February 1, 1632/3, *Statutes*, I, 208–209; "A Proposition concerning the winning of the Forrest," May 17, 1626, CO 1/4, f. 28; Harvey to [Privy Council], July 14, 1634, CO 1/8, f. 74; "Captain Thomas Yong's Voyage to Virginia and Delaware Bay and River in 1634," *Collections*, 111.

22. June 14, September 30, 1632, *Minutes*, 480; Harvey to Privy Council, February 20, 1632/3, CO 1/6, f. 195.

the governor noticed that his people were "more then ever resolved to make [Virginia] their Countrey" and earnestly requested the crown to encourage the emigration of skilled tradesmen to the colony, "especially shippwrights, smyths, carpenters, tanners, lether dressers, hemp dressers, and brickmakers and brick-layers: for now wee intent our houses for decency and Commodity."[23] The settlers were solely responsible for their modest prosperity, having created it through the production of tobacco and defended it by force of arms against the Indians. After suffering a devastating series of blows in the first year of the war they managed to defeat their enemy—or at least fight him to a draw—by creating and supporting a rudimentary paramilitary system tolerably well suited to the peculiar geographic, economic, and social conditions of the colony. By the end of the decade the new system was turning most of the colonists into reasonably well-trained militiamen capable of carrying out regular offensive operations against the Indians. John Smith must have been pleased.

The war demonstrated that Virginia's greatest economic asset—tobacco—was its greatest military liability. Tobacco caused the early planters to live in a widely dispersed pattern of settlement and to value their individual interests over the welfare of the community. The Virginia settler was determined to defend himself and his property if he could, but he was not inclined to participate in time-consuming offensive operations. Wyatt and his successors recognized this problem and were able to demonstrate to the settlers that under certain conditions military service would cause them little or no economic hardship. The laws passed in 1624 regulating service and compensation were the foundation of the early militia: they enabled Virginians to farm and fight effectively at the same time. When the war came to an end the militia was retained, reorganized, and strengthened. That the colony realized the need for a permanent military organization was fortunate, for the first major Anglo-Indian conflict in America failed to decide whether the natives or the newcomers would dominate tidewater Virginia. Another clash was inevitable.

23. Harvey to Privy Council, May 29, 1630, CO 1/5, ff. 203–204; governor and council to Privy Council, March 6, 1631/2, in Johnson, "Virginia in 1632," 465.

4. Virginia at War

In 1634 the colony was divided into eight counties, and the militia was reorganized along county lines.[1] The men of each county were formed into a company, and an officer called the lieutenant was appointed by the governor to command them. The new structure loosely paralleled the familiar English model. The post of county lieutenant, for example, was derived from the office of lord lieutenant back home, for the Virginia officer's responsibilities were described as being "the same as in England, and in a more especial manner to take care of the warr against Indians." The lieutenant was responsible for the training and equipping of his troops and was empowered to attack nearby Indians "as he shall finde occasion." The title of lieutenant never caught on, however, and the colonists continued to refer to their local military leaders as either commanders or captains.[2]

The militia officers of the 1630s and later were not the mercenaries and professional soldiers of an earlier day. Most were successful planters, aggressive, resourceful, and independent men who had battled nature, Indians, and each other to achieve their modest place and prosperity. Few had any military experience or training except perhaps in the English militia, but in the struggle against Opechancanough many displayed the energy and initiative vital to success in irregular warfare. Apparently, the traits that made a man an effective frontier entrepreneur might also make him an effective frontier officer. Militia offices in early Virginia were occupied by the "gentry" as they were in England, but many of these men also were stalwart soldiers. That they took their paramilitary responsibilities seriously is partially evidenced by the number and variety of English military manuals and histories purchased during the century. Well-thumbed copies of William Barriffe's *Military Discipline*, Robert Ward's *Animadversions of War*, Jonas Moore's *Mod-*

1. Portions of this chapter are reprinted from *Military Affairs*, October 1977, pp. 142–47, with permission. Copyright 1977 by the American Military Institute. No additional copies may be made without the express permission of the author and of the editor of *Military Affairs*.

2. September 4, 1632, 1634, *Statutes*, I, 193, 224.

ern Fortifications, and other books circulated among Virginia's amateur militia officers, who undoubtedly gleaned from them what seemed most appropriate for muster or march in the American wilderness.[3]

An incident that occurred in 1639 illustrates how the new decentralized county system worked. In July of that year some residents of Lower Norfolk County complained of being harassed by Indians. The county commander, Captain Adam Thoroughgood, thereupon called up fifteen "sufficient men" from his militia company and directed them to march out and chastise the guilty natives. Unlike the fifty-man companies of the military regime, county companies were not operational units. They normally served as reservoirs of trained manpower from which soldiers were drawn as needed. Each of the Lower Norfolk militiamen was supported in this enterprise by twenty county residents who pooled their resources and supplied him with two pounds of shot, two pounds of powder, forty pounds of biscuit, and half a bushel of peas. Residents also paid Cornelius Lloyd 250 pounds of tobacco for each of the seven new buff coats he provided for the protection of the militiamen. The fifteen men selected for the march did not have to pay for their provisions or coats, though they apparently were expected to furnish their own firearms and other weapons. While they were gone each of their farms and families was attended to by those same twenty "adjacent and inhabitinge neighbours." Everything proceeded smoothly except that, as always, a few slackers tried to avoid paying their share. William Shiff agreed with the other nineteen men in his support group that he would supply militiaman William Berry with the forty pounds of biscuit. The nineteen promised to pay Shiff twenty pounds of tobacco in return. Sometime later Shiff complained that he had not received the tobacco, and the county commissioners ordered the nineteen welshers to pay up immediately.[4]

3. Morgan, *American Slavery*, 123–30, 149; Bailyn, "Politics and Social Structure in Virginia," 90–115; Wright, *First Gentlemen*, 117–54; Bruce, *Institutional History*, I, 402–41; Davis, *Intellectual Life*, II, 491–595; Smart, "Private Libraries," 24–52.

4. July 17, 1639, March 2, 1639/40, April 12, 1641, Lower Norfolk County Records, Minute Book, 1637–46, ff. 35, 39, 99 (all county records are from microfilm in the Virginia State Library).

This affair was a typical small-scale county action of the period. It is also the earliest such operation of which a reasonably complete record has survived. (Unfortunately, the Lower Norfolk county clerk was so involved in keeping track of financial affairs on the home front he neglected to record what happened on the expedition.) It demonstrates that by 1639 and perhaps a few years earlier the principle of local responsibility was firmly established: the raw gentlemen and rugged farmers of each county company were largely on their own. The pattern of most local military activity for the rest of the century was set. This new system was an improvement over previous arrangements, but it contained two potentially serious weaknesses. For a decade after 1634 no mechanism existed to allow adjacent county forces to coordinate their activities in times of crisis. Local responsibility and the steady outward movement of the frontier also resulted in progressively less incentive for the older counties to maintain an effective military posture. After 1634 a smaller and smaller proportion of the population would bear the primary burden of defending the entire colony against Indians.

The reorganization into small units also turned up one very unsettling bit of information that would plague the militia for the rest of its existence. When the lieutenants first mustered their new companies for drill and inspection in 1634 they discovered there no longer were enough guns to go around. Without any statistics it is difficult to know how serious the situation really was, though hard usage, poor maintenance, and high humidity surely had taken a heavy toll of the old military equipment that had arrived in the colony before and during the war. The Virginians were sufficiently alarmed to beseech King Charles for another royal gift of arms from the Tower. It was "most requisite," argued Governor Harvey in 1634, that an ample supply of weaponry "be hastened hither, for although the Colony is better secured in the lower parts [below the recently completed palisade], yet the upper parts have many weak plantations, and the Indians, though yet upon faire termes, are alwayes to be doubted and ourselves prepared for them." Harvey repeated his plea for armaments and twice offered to purchase a thousand muskets and more than one hundred barrels of powder from the Tower. (He observed pointedly that the cost could be deducted from the

£4,000 the king owed him in back salary.) But his efforts were in vain. The crown was beset by mounting political problems at home and took little notice of faraway Virginia's pleas for help. In 1640 Jamestown gave up trying to solve the weapons shortage with royal largess and ordered all able-bodied freemen to follow the crown's earlier instructions and provide themselves and their white servants with "arms both offensive and defensive" within a year.[5] The burden of obtaining armaments was placed squarely on the shoulders of the population—a population that would grow increasingly distressed by the declining price of tobacco as the century progressed.

Ironically, the presence and not the absence of weapons may have posed the greater threat to the peace and quiet of early Virginia. An armed population occasionally proved difficult to govern, and more than one colonial executive found himself at the mercy of his aroused subjects. This unruliness was in part the result of the absence of a professional standing force that could be relied upon to maintain order and protect established authority. Virginia had no regulars or police force or palace guard. Instead, Virginia had an amateur, decentralized, paramilitary organization designed primarily to fight Indians, an organization that was actually the armed population in institutional form. To make matters worse, after 1634 the royal governors had little direct control over the militia or the armaments in its hands. In England the appointment of lords lieutenants a century earlier helped to give the crown a firm grip on men and arms in the countryside because the lieutenants were, first and foremost, the king's men. In Virginia the appointment of county commanders did not always have the same effect, for the commanders occasionally proved to be their own men.

The rebellion against John Harvey in 1635 demonstrated the governor's vulnerability to the use of armed force. The mutiny ap-

5. "Captain Thomas Yong's Voyage," *Collections*, 111; governor and council to Privy Council, February 8, 1633/4, CO 1/8, f. 9; Harvey's petition to the king [1638?], State Papers, 16/323, ff. 310–11; "Acts of the Generall Assembly," 147. Masters were not required to provide arms for black servants or slaves after 1640 but presumably could do so if they wished. Free blacks were members of the militia and were expected to arm themselves in the same fashion as whites (Breen and Innes, *"Myne Owne Ground,"* 25–27).

parently was caused by a bitter dispute between Harvey and the major planters (many of them councillors and commanders) over the validity of their property rights after the dissolution of the Virginia Company. In the midst of this crisis within the highest levels of government the province was swept by alarming rumors of an impending Indian assault. A visitor at Jamestown reported that the colony "is at this present full of rumors of warrs; for hither the countrey resorts dayly, from all parts, with newes that the Indians are gatheringe heade." In a bid for popular support, Harvey's opponents charged that the governor was responsible for Indian unrest because he had made "a daungerous peace" with Opechancanough in 1632 "against the Councells and Cuntreyes advice," a blunder that might lead to a second massacre. Thus many colonists believed their property and their lives to be in jeopardy and, rightly or wrongly, they blamed Harvey.[6]

Without any military force at his command Harvey was helpless against the rising tide of discontent. The end came at a stormy meeting in Jamestown, when one of the councillors told Harvey that "the peoples fury is up against you and to appease it, is beyond our power." A signal was given, and "straight about 40 Musketiers marched up to the doore of the Governors house" and arrested the astounded Harvey in his own parlor. Back in England a short time later the former governor explained how his enemies "caused Guards to bee sett in all ways and passages so that no man could travell or come from place to place," and he ruefully acknowledged that he had no "meanes or power to raise any force to suppress this mutiny, they having restrayned me, and sett a guard upon me."[7]

Government in early Virginia depended on the tacit consent of the governed, for the governed had the means to resist authority. As long as the population was armed and the militia remained the only effective military force in the province, and as long as direct control of the militia remained in the hands of local authorities,

6. Thornton, "Thrusting Out of Governor Harvey," 11–26; "Captain Thomas Yong's Voyage," *Collections*, 113; Samuel Mathews to Sir John Wotslenholme, May 25, 1635, CO 1/8, f. 178; Richard Kemp to commissioners for plantations, May 17, 1635, CO 1/8, f. 166.

7. Kemp to commissioners, May 17, 1635, CO 1/8, f. 167; "Declaration of Sir John Harvey to the Lords Commissioners for Foreign Plantations" [1635], *ibid.*, p. 197.

rulers had to live with the specter of revolt. On the evening John Harvey unceremoniously lost his job, a settler was asked by a recently arrived visitor why he was carrying a musket so near the governor's residence. "Tis noe matter," the musketeer replied, "he shall know wee have armes."[8] Harvey was the first but not the last of Virginia's royal governors to experience the meaning of those words.

The armistice with Opechancanough lasted twelve years, but they were not peaceful years. There were skirmishes and punitive raids nearly every year between 1632 and 1644. The tense atmosphere enabled the postwar governors to maintain and in some cases improve the colony's defensive posture. Before being abruptly "thrust out of his Government" Harvey presided over the reorganization and decentralization of the militia, tried to obtain additional arms from England, and even planned to secure the entire peninsula by erecting a second palisade about thirty miles above the first. His successor, Sir Francis Wyatt, served as an interim governor and made no major changes in the militia during his brief stay. Wyatt seems to have been satisfied with the current state of the forces he had done so much to create during the war. In any case, he was preoccupied with domestic problems and reported his time was "wholy taken up" with plans to raise tobacco prices.[9]

Wyatt was relieved in 1642 just as the truce with the Indians began to break down. By the time Sir William Berkeley arrived at Jamestown the number of violent incidents flaring along the frontier had increased noticeably. Threatened counties responded in various ways. The commander of Northampton County, for example, warned his people of the "greate and suddayne daynger which is like to come upon the Plantation by the Indians" and announced that any men found "abroad from theire dwellings and Plantations without theire gunns fixed and a quantitye of powder and shott with them" would be penalized. (Seven persons caught outdoors without arms shortly thereafter were sentenced to "Cutt up all the

8. Washburn, *Governor and the Rebel*, 20; Kemp to commissioners, May 17, 1635, CO 1/8, f. 167.

9. Richard Kemp to Sir Francis Windebanke, April 6, 1638, CO 1/9, f. 228; April 28, 1635, *Minutes*, 481; Wyatt to [?], March 25, 1640, CO 1/10, f. 162.

Weedes" around the parish church.) In Northampton and several other counties militia companies were mustered in a show of force apparently intended to impress nearby Indians with English might and preparedness, and a small detachment of troops was sent to help the Marylanders deal with some tribes north of the Potomac—an early and rare instance of intercolonial aid.[10]

Alarmed by the deteriorating situation, Governor Berkeley began to prepare the colony for the worst. His military instructions from the Privy Council required him only to call up the militia four times a year for drill and review and in general to follow "the Course practised in the Realm of England." Berkeley fortunately realized that English rules did not apply in the New World, and he ordered a threefold increase in training and a general upgrading of the militia. Every commander was instructed to provide his unit with a signal drum, headquarters field tent, and flags "with all convenient expedition" and to be "very carefull to exercise and trayne his Company *once evrye Month or Oftener*." The names of absentees and slackers now were to be sent directly to Jamestown, where punishment presumably would involve more than hacking weeds.[11]

Berkeley also tried to halt and even reverse the deadly flow of firearms into Indian hands. One of the greatest military advantages held by the English in Virginia was their light body armor, a miscellaneous assortment of plate, mail, brigandines, jacks, and buff coats. Such equipment, however, offered little protection against firearms. Laws against passing arms and ammunition to the enemy were not always observed. Some settlers actually sold weapons to the natives; others hired Indian hunters and furnished them with "peeces, powder and shott, by which great abuse, not onely the Indians (to the great indangering of the collony) are instructed in the use of our arms, But have opportunity given them to store themselves as well with arms as powder and shott." This situation was intolerable, and in 1643 the assembly ordered that anyone found

10. October 5, 1642, *Minutes*, 499; April 28, 1643, August 2, 1641, January 3, 1642/3, in Ames, *County Court Records of Accomack-Northampton, 1640–1645*, 268, 105, 235; Scisco, "Evolution of Colonial Militia in Maryland," 169.

11. Instructions to Berkeley, August, 1641, CO 5/1354, ff. 229–30; commission to Francis Yeardley, July 2, 1642, in Ames, *County Court Records of Accomack-Northampton, 1640–1645*, 176–77.

selling, trading, giving, or loaning arms and ammunition to the natives would be severely punished. Moreover, in an attempt to undo the damage that already had been done, the assembly authorized any settler who came upon an armed Indian in the woods to seize and disarm him, if at all possible, and keep the gun.[12] Such action surely could not have improved Anglo-Indian relations.

It may have been at this time that Berkeley chose to build or begin building the brick tower that still stands in the middle of Jamestown. This massive three-story structure served as an entranceway and bell tower for a stout brick church, but it seems to have been constructed with another purpose in mind, for it has six loopholes or gunports on the third floor. The tower and church together may have been considered a garrison house or "keep" into which the residents of Jamestown could retire if the Indians overran their settlement. Musketeers could maintain a steady fire upon any intruders from high in the tower while women, children, and wounded huddled below in the church.[13]

By 1644 the militia had been reorganized into county companies and was preparing for a possible reopening of hostilities with the Indians. Some of the settler-soldiers were unarmed and others, generally newcomers, were inexperienced or unreliable, but a great many were veterans who had fought in the first war or in the numerous skirmishes that punctuated the cease-fire. The situation seemed stable enough for the moment, and the colonists turned their attention to the crucial task of spring planting. It was then that Opechancanough began the last phase of the struggle for tidewater Virginia.

On April 18, 1644, the tribes of the Powhatan confederation made a final, convulsive effort to drive the English from their land. In a devastating surprise attack thousands of Indian warriors fell upon Virginia's outlying farms and hamlets, killing nearly five hundred settlers in a single day and causing hundreds more to flee in terror toward the palisade and the older portions of the colony. The col-

12. March 2, 1642/43, *Statutes*, I, 255–56.

13. Jamestown had long outgrown its old palisade. See Cotter, *Archeological Excavations at Jamestown*, 21; Forman, *Jamestown and St. Mary's*, 153–54; Yonge, *Site of Old "James Towne,"* 65–66, 72–73.

ony's frontiers crumpled inward under the force of the blow. Strangely, the Indians failed to follow up their initial success and withdrew into the forests.[14]

No one will ever know why Opechancanough chose such a desperate, almost hopeless, course of action. His shrunken confederacy had lost the great numerical superiority it once enjoyed. Indeed, the Indians probably were outnumbered by the eight thousand or more colonists now residing in Virginia. An anonymous writer—possibly Berkeley—later suggested that Opechancanough was clever enough to recognize the opportunity presented to his people by the eruption of the English Civil War in 1642. It was rumored that some colonists had informed the old chief "that all was under the Sword in England, in their Native Countrey, and such divisions in our Land; That now was his time or never, to roote out all the English; For those that they could not surprize and kill under the feigned masque of Friendship and feasting, and the rest would be by wants; and having no supplyes from their own Countrey which could not helpe them, be suddenly Consumed and Famished." If true, this might explain the strange passivity of the Indians after their surprise attack: they were waiting for the colonists to starve.[15]

The attack itself was spectacularly successful because this time—unlike 1622—the settlers received no warning and therefore Virginia's paramilitary force was not deployed for battle. The provincial militia was not a force in being but a segment of the population designed to be mobilized in response to an immediate and specific threat or the actual outbreak of hostilities. The reactive nature of the Virginia militia—or of any militia—virtually conceded the first blow to the enemy. The real test of a militia's effectiveness was its ability to perform after the initial shock. The primary difficulty would be the confusion caused by an Indian attack;

14. February 17, 1644/5, October 1, 1644, *Statutes*, I, 290, 285–86; Beverley, *History and Present State of Virginia*, 60–61; [William Berkeley], *A Perfect Description of Virginia: Being, A full and true Relation of the present State of the Plantation* (London, 1649), *Tracts*, II, 11. The only other published account of the conflict is Shea, "Virginia at War," 142–47.

15. Morgan, *American Slavery*, 180, 404; [Berkeley], *Perfect Description*, *Tracts*, II, 11; Lurie, "Indian Cultural Adjustment," 50–52. An alternate explanation of the lull is Earle, "Environment, Disease, and Mortality," 107.

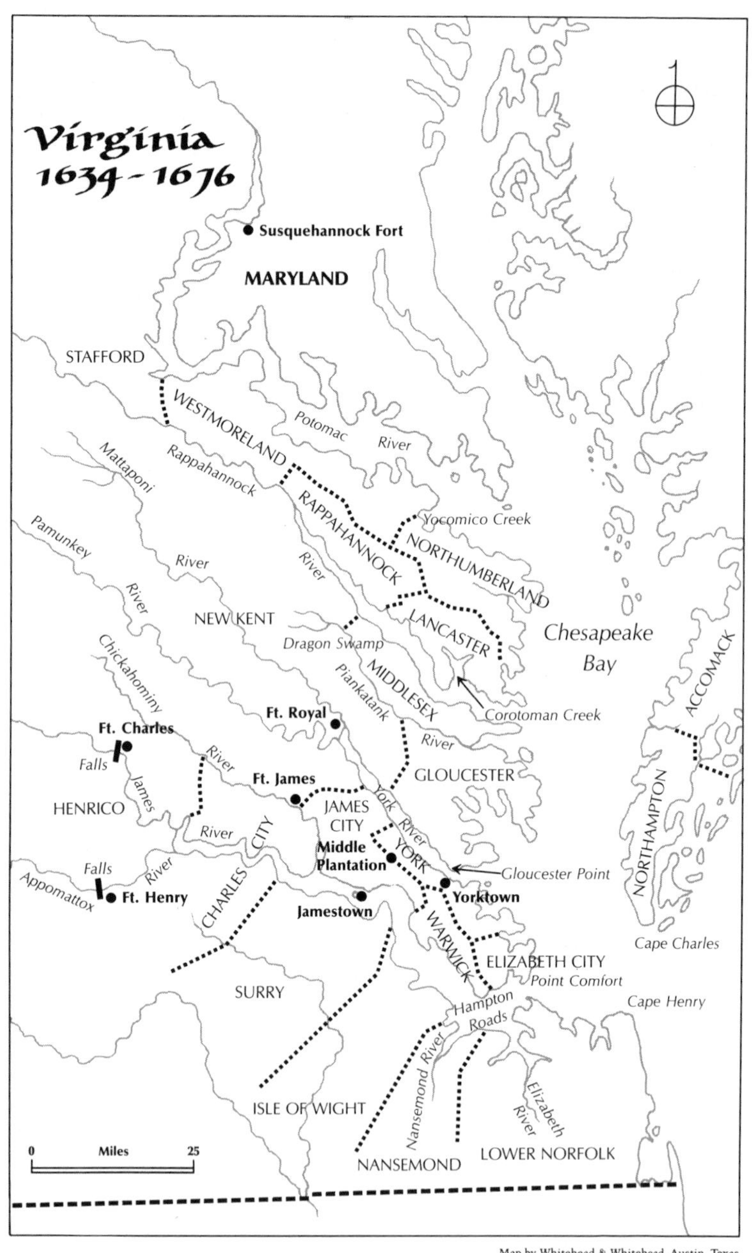

Map by Whitehead & Whitehead, Austin, Texas

under such chaotic conditions it would take time to muster stunned local troops or bring forces to the scene from adjacent counties. The scattered farms and primitive overland communications in tidewater Virginia aggravated these problems. Thus in the spring of 1644 the colonists were concerned and reasonably alert but had no idea the natives were preparing an attack of such scope and intensity. Considering these drawbacks, the strength and rapidity of the English recovery is impressive.

The 1644 massacre dealt the Virginians a heavy blow, and the lull that followed was a great relief to them. The Indians had burned away the outer fringe of settlement. The most serious damage occurred along the south bank of the James and on the peninsula above the palisade. The only frontier area that had not yet been attacked was the Eastern Shore, and Berkeley sent the Northampton commander an "expresse order" to reduce his "stragling and Remote Plantations into Convenient and defensive bodyes" as quickly as possible. In the weeks that followed authorities at all levels labored to bolster defenses and prepare the militia for offensive operations. The Indians apparently made no effort to penetrate the somewhat decrepit old wall, but Berkeley took no chances. Eighty militiamen from York and James City counties were dispatched for "defense of the forest" to the tiny garrison-settlement of Middle Plantation. The governor and councillors also tried to relocate widowed and orphaned survivors of the massacre, drew up "particular directions for marching against the indians," and punished one unfortunate settler for using "improper language in time of war."[16]

The assembly convened at Jamestown in June and declared that because the natives once again had shown their true colors, "wee will for ever abandon all formes of peace and familiarity with the whole Nation, and will to the uttmost of our power pursue and root out those which have any way had theire hands in the shedding of our blood and Massacring of our People." All agreed that the tactics which had proved effective in the past should be fol-

16. [Berkeley], *Perfect Description*, *Tracts*, II, 11; Beverley, *History and Present State of Virginia*, 60–61; April 30, May, June, 1644, *Minutes*, 501–502; April 30, 1644, in Ames, *County Court Records of Accomack-Northampton, 1640–1645*, 359–60.

lowed "as farre as our abilityes and Ammunition shall enable us."[17]

Puzzled and relieved by the lack of enemy activity, the Virginians decided to launch their own offensive in late June. It was directed primarily against Opechancanough's stronghold at Pamunkey. Berkeley appointed Captain William Claiborne the "Generall and Chief Comannder" of the upcoming operation and granted him sweeping powers "to press and take such men and such necessaryes at the publique Charge as shall be expedient for the service." All civil and military officials in the colony were instructed to assist him in every possible way. Claiborne received such extraordinary authority because Berkeley was about to leave for England on a quest for military aid. For him to depart at such a critical time was strange (and it is unclear what help he expected from an England locked in civil war), but the governor sailed away confident that in his absence the directon of Virginia's initial offensive moves would be in capable hands.[18]

His confidence was not misplaced. Commanders of the seven counties participating in the planned march exercised "great Care" in choosing and outfitting their best men for the job. James City, Isle of Wight, and York counties each contributed fifty men, Elizabeth City and Lower Norfolk counties forty men each, and Warwick and Northampton counties thirty-five men each. Each of these three hundred soldiers was equipped with one pound of powder, four pounds of lead or pewter shot, "one good fixed Gunne and some defensive Coat or Armour and head piece with a sword or Cutlace and three weekes provision of Victualls." The counties provided boats to ferry their militiamen and supplies to Chiskiack, the rendezvous point, and from there to the place of battle. More than thirty horses "with theire furniture and roapes to tye them" were used as pack animals, apparently the first time this was done. The provincial government appointed one Henry Luellin to the post of "Chirurgeon Generall" for the army and ordered that "Mr. Cleverio or some other Minister bee entreated to bestowe his paynes with them." Armed to the teeth and provided with the best medi-

17. June 1, 1644, "Acts, Orders and Resolutions," 229–30.
18. *Ibid.*, 230–32; June 29, 1644, *Minutes*, 501; June 3, 1644, *JHB*, I, 71.

cal and religious assistance available, Claiborne's little army prepared to move out, every man undoubtedly comforted by the promise that should he be wounded or injured on the march he would be "mayntained by the Country, And in Case any shall bee slayne, All possible Care shall be taken of theire estates and of theire widdowes and Children."[19]

The "Pamunky army" left Chiskiack at the end of June and sailed up the York River toward the enemy. It then dropped out of sight. No account of the campaign has survived, but it is known from indirect evidence that the English "landed against the Indians" at Pamunkey, destroyed towns and cornfields, and pursued Opechancanough and his people into the interior. In early August the weary little army returned to Chiskiack and disbanded.[20]

The Pamunkey offensive was the main thrust of a three-pronged campaign. While Claiborne's troops went into action along the York the residents of Upper Norfolk (Nansemond) County attacked natives in their area, a move apparently designed to relieve pressure on the exposed southern frontier. Meanwhile, militiamen of the two beleaguered counties above the palisade, Charles City and Henrico, struggled as best they could "against all theire Neighboring Indians" in order to "divert them from Pomunckey as farre as theire Ammunition and Abilityes will enable them." A diversion was all that could be expected from these counties because they had suffered heavy casualties in the massacre, and Jamestown promised them increased aid as soon as the Pamunkey march was completed.[21]

Little is known about this first series of offensive operations, but it is clear that considerable damage was done to Indian towns and crops, particularly those of the Pamunkeys. The most interesting aspect of the campaign was the unusual degree of specialization and coordination among the three task forces: a single-county holding action south of the James, a modest diversion above the palisade, and a powerful attack against the main enemy strong-

19. [1644], "Acts, Orders and Resolutions," 231–34.
20. June 29, July 6, August 5, October 15, 1644, *Minutes*, 501–502; June 22, 1644, in Clifford, "Some Recently Discovered Extracts," 66–67.
21. [1644], "Acts, Orders and Resolutions," 230–31.

hold. The disproportionately large size of the last force reflected the widespread belief that the Indians could not or would not carry on the war without Opechancanough. But the old chief and his tribesmen had only been driven deeper into the forests; they had not been destroyed.

Having seized the initiative the colonists tried to keep up the pressure. Upon learning of Claiborne's safe return, Acting Governor Richard Kemp and the council sent fifty troops as promised to aid the undermanned militia companies of Charles City and Henrico counties in a raid against the Chickahominies. Thereafter, smaller parties were dispatched at regular intervals in all directions to destroy Indian cornfields and stores of food. The onset of winter eventually halted the fighting.[22]

The assembly met again early in 1645 and instituted several administrative and tactical changes. To allow greater flexibility in dealing with the enemy, Virginia was divided into two military associations or districts. The three counties located south of the James River were brought temporarily under the authority of a "counsell of warr" composed of the three commanders and their deputies. The southside council was subordinate only to the governor and was empowered to levy troops, arms, ammunition, and other supplies "as emergencie of occasions shall require." Provincial authorities at Jamestown served as the council of war for the other military association, which was composed of the peninsular counties and the Eastern Shore. Under this new arrangement local responsibility apparently was expanded to include the entire association and not just the individual county. Contemporaries generally thought this to be the "most convenient" way to "extirpate and subdue this people that doe much annoy us."[23]

The peninsular counties or northside association faced a peculiar situation. The successful expeditions against the Pamunkeys, Chickahominies, and other tribes had driven those natives so far away they had become only a distant threat. With a large area beyond the palisade cleared of hostile forces, a change in tactics seemed in order to prevent the enemy from creeping back down the pen-

22. August 5, September 3, October 23, November 26, December, 1644, January 20, 1644/5, *Minutes*, 501–502.

23. February 17, 1644/5, *Statutes*, I, 292; Frank, "News from Virginny," 85.

insula unmolested and undetected. Officials at Jamestown therefore devised a novel plan to secure the upper peninsula and facilitate future military operations in that area. The association would build and garrison a string of frontier forts stretching from the falls of the James River eastward to the head of the York River.[24]

Three small forts were erected in the spring of 1645: Fort Royal near the ruins of the Pamunkey villages, Fort Charles by the falls of the James (now Richmond), and Fort James "on the Ridge of Chiquohomine" midway between the other two posts. About a hundred men were assigned to these palisaded blockhouses. Their duty was twofold. First, they were to try to prevent Indian raiding parties from moving down the peninsula toward the palisade some forty to sixty miles below. Second, whenever the opportunity presented itself, the three groups were to join forces and move against Opechancanough and the Pamunkeys. If, in such a case, "they shall not be thought a sufficient company so joyned," Jamestown would immediately muster more troops to reinforce them on the march.[25]

Kemp ordered every fifteen tithables in his association to "sett forth, compleatly furnish and maintain" one settler for the garrison force needed to man the forts. Unlike militiamen, who served without pay as a civic duty, each of these soldiers enlisted for a specific term of duty up to a year at a "sallary" agreed upon with the other fourteen members of his group. If no one in a particular group wanted to volunteer, the northside council of war could "press whom they shall think fitt," and if financial negotiations broke down, the council would "allow the soldier such satisfaction from the 14 as to them shall seem convenient." Each soldier was armed and provided "with all necessaries" by the members of his group but was responsible for reimbursing the owners of the weapons "in case he shall negligently loose or spoyle them." If a garrison soldier was killed, his salary was due to his family, if any; if a soldier was injured, all medical and welfare costs were to be borne by his home county.[26]

The creation of the garrison force was an early sign of another

24. February 17, 1644/5, *Statutes*, I, 292–93.
25. *Ibid.*, 293.
26. *Ibid.*, 292–93. A similar development in neighboring Maryland is discussed in Carr and Menard, "Immigration and Opportunity," 218, 231.

slight but disturbing trend within the Virginia militia: the tendency to allow an ever greater share of military responsibility to devolve on an ever smaller segment of the population. The men recruited in 1645 were paid a sum of money to serve a lengthy term of duty on the frontier. They were neither indentured servants nor established planters, for the former could not forsake their valuable labor and the latter would not abandon their hard-won financial interests. Thus many of the garrison troops must have been poor freemen who had no regular income and little or no economic stake in the community. Most likely they were young, landless men to whom a fixed "sallary" and a chance for adventure seemed more attractive than endless drudgery as a tenant or hired laborer. If this was the makeup of the troops, it may explain why the north-side council of war took the unusual step of ordering the other fourteen members of each group to see that their soldier had the proper arms, while cautioning the soldier about the rights and responsibilities of using borrowed private property. And, of course, it made good sense to garrison a string of isolated outposts with expendable young men who had no pressing economic or familial need to remain within the settled areas. Nevertheless, the result was that a small group of Virginians was being hired to shoulder the military burdens of a great many others, an ominous development for the militia and the colony as a whole. By the end of the century this practice had become standard.

While the forts were under construction Governor Berkeley returned to Virginia with the news that no help could be expected from the embattled royal faction in England. The gloom that followed this announcement was dispelled a few days later when a letter arrived at Jamestown from Margaret Worleigh, a captive of the Pamunkeys. She informed the governor that Opechancanough desired an exchange of prisoners and an end to the war. After some consideration the Virginians decided to set a trap for Opechancanough just as Wyatt and Tucker had done two decades earlier. Berkeley declared a temporary truce and agreed to meet with Indian leaders in June at Fort Royal. It was a ruse. When a group of chiefs and warriors approached the fort on the appointed day, the gates suddenly flew open and the garrison made a "hot charge" upon the startled Indians. Quite a few were killed or captured, but Opechancanough escaped in the confusion. This success inspired a new series of raids for the "cutting upp of the Indians Corne," which lasted until winter closed the second season of campaigning.[27]

The assembly met again in the spring of 1646 after another relatively peaceful winter. Authorities were so pleased with the forts they decided to add a fourth outpost, Fort Henry, at the falls of the Appomattox River (now Petersburg). The forty-five-man garrison enlisted on the same terms as the soldiers at the other posts. To help secure the long, exposed frontier below the fort, the southside council of war announced that "all persons whatsoever . . . for their safeguard and defense from the savages, according to the number of people in their families, were proportionally allotted to set out and maintain men in manner of a scout." Little is known about these earliest "scouts" or rangers except that they served for pay on a contract basis much like the garrison forces.[28]

The gradual shift to a more passive defense on both sides of the James probably was caused by "the great and vast expence" of waging a prolonged and inconclusive war. In an attempt to end the conflict as quickly and inexpensively as possible, the assembly decided to raise a force of sixty northside militiamen to track down Opechancanough and kill him or force him to terms. All other operations were suspended as the troops slipped downriver from Kecoughtan, sailed up the York to Fort Royal, and disappeared into the wilderness.[29]

What happened next is unclear. Evidence is very scanty, but it seems that the expedition soon stumbled across the trail of the Pamunkeys and so informed the governor. Berkeley responded by forming "a Party of Horse" and personally leading it on "a speedy March" to join in the pursuit. The fleeing Pamunkeys were hin-

27. July, August, September, 1645, in Clifford, "Some Recently Discovered Extracts," 69; May 25, 1648, York County Records, No. 2, Wills and Deeds, 1645–49, p. 361; *A Description of the Province of New Albion* (London, 1648), *Tracts*, II, 6.

28. March 2, 1645/6, *Statutes*, I, 315; November 3, 1645, Lower Norfolk County Records, Minute Book, 1637–46, ff. 85, 87.

29. March 2, 1645/6, *Statutes*, I, 317–19.

dered by the aged and feeble Opechancanough, who had to be carried on a litter. Berkeley's fast-moving mounted troops surprised the Indians and captured Opechancanough without much resistance. The old chief was brought back to Jamestown a prisoner, and there "by the Governour's Command, he was treated with all the Respect and Tenderness imaginable. . . . However, he could not preserve his Life above a Fortnight; For one of the Soldiers, resenting the Calamities the Colony had suffer'd by this Prince's Means, basely shot him thro' the Back, after he was made Prisoner; of which Wound he died. He continued brave to the last Moment of his Life," concluded Robert Beverley's famous account, "and show'd not the least Dejection at his Captivity."[30] Thus did the settlers' most implacable foe meet his end.

The death of "that bloody Monster" Opechancanough led to the surrender of the Powhatan confederation and associated tribes in October, 1646. A treaty was signed wherein the Indians ceded the south side and the peninsula to the English and promised to return all "negroes and guns" in their possession. The confederation was broken up, and the various tribes agreed to be loyal subjects and allies of the crown. For their part, the English promised to protect the grievously weakened tribes against their traditional enemies to the west and north.[31]

The treaty also included an innovative scheme to reduce friction by dividing tidewater Virginia into distinct English and Indian districts in which only members of one group or the other could reside, work, hunt, fish, or travel. Contact between colonists and natives was drastically limited, and any Indian found within the English zone could be shot on sight unless he was a messenger to the governor wearing "a coate of striped stuffe" as identification and a guarantee of safe conduct. The settlers, however, retained the right to expand their area at the Indians' expense whenever they wished to do so. Thus the reservation system in America was born

30. Beverley, *History and Present State of Virginia*, 60–62; [Berkeley], *Perfect Description, Tracts*, II, 7; *Description of the Province, Tracts*, II, 6.

31. [Berkeley], *Perfect Description, Tracts*, II, 7; October 5, 1646, *Statutes*, I, 323–26; Craven, "Indian Policy," 75–78.

complete with the loophole that was to sabotage most attempts to guarantee defeated tribes productive lands of their own.[32]

After approving the treaty the assembly set about partially dismantling Virginia's military machine, such as it was, thereby initiating a national tradition. The militia was retained in its current form, but the garrisons and scouts were disbanded. The number of annual training sessions was reduced, and the forts were turned over to private interests who agreed to maintain them in return for a grant of "a competent quantity of land" and limited exemption from taxation. The regular garrisons occupied the posts until the end of 1646 and then were paid for their services and sent home.[33] Two years and eight months after the second great massacre Virginia was at peace for the first time in twenty-four years.

The Second Tidewater War had relatively little impact on the everyday affairs of most settlers for it was fought along and beyond the frontier. In the first conflict, particularly during 1622 and 1623, the Indian onslaught nearly precipitated the collapse of the colony by annihilating a huge portion of the population and forcing the abandonment of most of the settled areas, thereby causing a famine and a disastrous epidemic. During that long decade many colonists lived in constant fear of an attack. Two decades later the situation had changed considerably, partly as a result of lessons learned at a bitter cost in the first war. By 1644 Virginia had perhaps ten times as many people spread over a larger territory, much of it secure from Indian attack, and possessed a well-organized paramilitary force with some combat experience. Both people and institutions were better prepared to withstand the grueling strains of war. In 1622 the natives attacked a pathetic little outpost unable to survive without aid from England; twenty years later they took on a maturing colonial society capable of defending itself.

During the hostilities life went on in a fairly routine manner except for active militiamen, garrison troops, and scouts. The colonists naturally behaved more cautiously during such "dangerous

32. October 5, 1646, *Statutes*, I, 323–26.
33. *Ibid.*, 326–29.

times," and just after the massacre even those living within the palisade were reluctant "to goe over the forrest alone." By October, 1644, confidence had been largely restored. Refugees began to return to their frontier homes, and a telltale epidemic of "carelesse stragling" broke out.[34]

Except for the massacre the casualty rate was extremely low, even among active militiamen, a sign that the Indians were willing to lose their towns and crops rather than resist armored English raiders. None of the five hundred troops engaged in the combined operations of 1644 were killed, and only a small number were "hurt and maymed and disabled from provideing for their necessary maintenance and subsistence." Those unlucky soldiers who did suffer injuries were nursed back to health at public expense as promised and occasionally were granted special privileges. For example, the Northumberland County court in 1653 permanently exempted one John Johnson from all county and provincial taxes "in respect of his lameness and inability to worke which was contracted in the service of the Country in the last Massacre."[35] In general, it seems that after the terrible spring of 1644 the average Virginian whether at home or on the march was relatively safe from bodily harm.

Eventually, the financial strain began to tell, which may explain why the colonists were so anxious to see the war end in 1646. Inhabitants of each county were responsible for "all charges and disbursements for the cure of hurt men or horses or for boats lost and damnified, boats hire[d], provision or ammunition imployed in the publique service or any other charge." The southside association spent over thirty-eight thousand pounds of tobacco on military purposes in 1645, a figure that does not include the private financial arrangements made to support the scouts and Fort Henry's garrison. The rate of taxation had grown so onerous by November, 1645 that the assembly concluded that the traditional method of

34. October 1, 1644, February 17, 1644/5, November 20, 1645, *ibid.*, 285–86, 291, 298, 300–301; [1644], York County Records, No. 2, Wills and Deeds, 1645–49, p. 117.

35. October 1, 1644, March 2, 1645/6, *Statutes*, I, 287, 285, 311; October 30, 1645, Lower Norfolk County Records, Minute Book, 1637–46, f. 84; May 20, 1653, Northumberland County Records, Record Book, 1652–58, p. 13.

levying taxes had become "insupportable for the poorer sorte to beare" and replaced it with a graduated tax based on the visible wealth of the individual. Moreover, because "the earnest prosecution of the present warrs hath subjected this collony to an excessive charge," members of the council, who normally were exempt from all taxation, henceforth contributed their fair share along with everyone else.[36]

Most Virginians of both high and low status apparently supported the war effort as best they could. There were only a few attempts to deprive militiamen of their legal rights, and they were uniformly unsuccessful. A fairly typical incident involved Robert Lewis of York County, who was called up for the final expedition in 1646. Four of Lewis' neighbors neglected to perform "duly and exactly" their appointed amount of work on his farm. After Lewis complained, the northside council of war fined each delinquent one hundred pounds of tobacco and ordered each to labor in the militiaman's fields for six full days. There also were a few attempts to welsh on private agreements. One Nicholas Sebriell failed to provide his share of a "souldiers wages and diett" at Fort Royal. He later was ordered to pay the enlistee three hundred pounds of tobacco and one barrel of corn and to bear court costs. All in all, considering the large number of men called up for military service and the heavy expense of supporting the salaried troops, the incidence of cheating and bad faith was minimal. The self-seeking individualism that characterized early Virginia failed to subvert the militia system during this crisis.[37]

The Second Tidewater War was the high point in the military history of seventeenth-century Virginia. Never again would the militia perform so well or achieve such an overwhelming victory. The conflict was seen as a kind of holy war against the deadliest enemy, indeed, the only enemy, most Virginians had ever known.

36. October 30, 1645, Lower Norfolk County Records, Minute Book, 1637–46, f. 84; Frank, "News from Virginny," 85; October 1, 1644, November 20, 1645, *Statutes*, I, 285, 287–88, 305–307.

37. December 21, November 26, 1646, January 27, 1646/7, York County Records, No. 2, Wills and Deeds, 1645–49, pp. 197, 192, 210. The currently accepted view of early Chesapeake society is ably presented in Breen and Innes, *"Myne Owne Ground,"* 56–57.

A sense of common purpose seems to have united the settlers and spared them from becoming embroiled in social and political turmoil such as was wracking England. Internal differences were put aside for a little while. "We are at peace among ourselves," wrote a Virginian in 1645, "and have beene so ever since the massacre."[38] Alas, such unity would not last.

38. Frank, "News from Virginny," 85.

5. Innovations and Invasions

During the next thirty years the course of military affairs in Virginia was heavily influenced by developments in England. When Parliament, Oliver Cromwell, and Charles II attempted in various ways to revitalize the moribund national militia between 1648 and 1664, their efforts had a significant if unintended impact in the Old Dominion. As colonials often do, the Virginians sought to emulate what was happening back home by remodeling their own paramilitary forces. In 1652 a regiment was created in each county in place of the venerable company. A typical regiment consisted of eight or ten companies of foot, that is, infantry. The simple county command structure established in 1634 was enlarged to include a regimental colonel (presumably the former county commander), a lieutenant colonel, a major, several captains, and assorted junior officers. In English fashion the eight or ten senior officers in each regiment commanded the individual companies. These officers were expected to muster and drill their men "in the use of their armes [and] postures of war" at least twice a year "or oftener upon Command, or emergent causes." In every county a small body of prominent local men, usually including some of the ranking officers of the regiment, was organized to oversee paramilitary operations. These men were known as commissioners of the militia. There were two minor exceptions to this structure: the Charles City and Henrico militia were combined into a single regiment, and the militia in populous York County was divided into two regiments.[1]

Not long after this reorganization had taken place, fear of an Indian attack caused the commissioners of the Charles City–Henrico regiment to make further changes on their own. They decreed that in the event a "warre should breake forth" fifty men on each side

1. Western, *English Militia*, 5–16; Billings, "Some Acts Not in Hening's *Statutes*," 30–31; November 20, 1654, *Statutes*, I, 387; March 24, 1655, *JHB*, I, 95; September 17, 1655, Charles City County Records, 1655–65, pp. 20–21. A 1652 ordinance contains the first known use of the word "militia" in an official Virginia document (Billings, "Some Acts Not in Hening's *Statutes*," 30–31).

of the James River should be prepared "to be in readinesse at an howers warning with their armes and 12 shott of powder and ball a man." If the Indians struck, these little bands would assemble and march to the sound of the guns. The danger of an immediate attack soon passed, but this novel arrangement seemed so sensible it was renewed a year later. The appearance along the upper James of these "trainbands," a misnomer apparently inherited in garbled fashion from Elizabethan times, marks the beginning of permanent functional specialization within the militia. It also reflects the fact that the harsh demands of the American environment continued to interact with English traditions and contemporary developments in the fashioning of the provincial forces.[2]

In 1661 the Virginians made additional far-reaching changes in their paramilitary institution. The Charles City–Henrico innovation proved to be so attractive the government ordered three small "trainbands" created within each regiment. Members of these units were expected to be "always ready in armes" and prepared to march "to the rescue of such distressed places or persons as he their Commander shall direct." Because of the recent turmoil in England and the growing restlessness of Virginia's laboring class, militia officers were instructed to select only "freemen or servants of undoubted Fidelity" for this critical duty. As an afterthought a regimental troop of horse or dragoons was formed in each county to support the bands. Apparently for the first time the militia formally included mounted forces, though horsemen had been used successfully against Opechancanough in 1646.[3] The mounted arm of the militia would play an increasingly dominant role as the century progressed.

The authorities also dealt with "the unsetlednesse of the militia, the uncerteinties of Allarmes, and the want of fixed armes" at this time. Absenteeism had become a problem, and county officials complained that "divers refractory persons . . . to the ruyne of all military discipline refused to appeare upon the dayes of exercise and other times when required to attend upon the publique ser-

2. July 25, 1656, June 24, 1657, Charles City County Records, 1655–65, pp. 61, 102. An excellent synopsis of this development in another area is Billings, "English Legal Literature," 415.

3. July 15, 1661, Charles City County Records, 1655–65, pp. 279–80.

vice." The assembly ordered militia officers to fine delinquents one hundred pounds of tobacco for each unexcused absence. False alarms and rumors of Indian attacks were another source of concern. From time to time during the 1650s the colony fairly buzzed with wild predictions of imminent disaster, though most provincial officials believed that because of the "inconsiderable number of neighboring Indians" a major surprise attack was most unlikely and were puzzled by the "feares and terrors" of the general population. Of more immediate concern was the "frequent shooting of gunns in drinking," because whenever several shots were fired everyone within hearing distance assumed the Indians were attacking and acted accordingly. At first the assembly fined offenders one hundred pounds of tobacco. When this modest penalty failed to have much impact it was increased to five thousand pounds of tobacco and a year in jail. These actions must have had the desired effect for considerably less was heard of absenteeism and false alarms.[4]

The vexing, chronic shortage of arms and ammunition proved far more difficult to resolve. Every militiaman in the 1660s was required by law to have a gun in good working order and an ample supply of powder and shot. Unfortunately, a "diligent search and inquiry" revealed that relatively few Virginians were in full compliance with the law. As the economy of the tobacco coast slowed after mid-century, the Old Dominion's hard-pressed planters were not inclined to spend precious pounds and shillings to replace or repair military equipment. Perhaps recognizing that the combination of peace and hard times had made weaponry a low-priority item, provincial authorities allowed settlers with "unserviceable armes" to have them repaired at government expense and insisted only that trainbandsmen be fully armed.[5]

The only surviving account of a seventeenth-century Virginia militia muster describes how some of these changes were implemented at the local level. In July, 1661, the militia commissioners

4. *Ibid.*, 279–83; November 22, 1654, *Minutes*, 504; March 10, 1655/6, March 13, 1657/8, October 23, 1666, *Statutes*, I, 401–402, 480, II, 246–47.

5. "Extracts from Proceedings of the House of Burgesses," 388–89; March 10, 1655/6, March 1–15, 1658/9, March 23, 1661/2, *Statutes*, I, 399, 525, II, 126–27; July 15, 1661, Charles City County Records, 1655–65, p. 279; Carr and Menard, "Immigration and Opportunity," 237.

of Charles City and Henrico counties met at Westover to put the new directives into effect. They had less to do than other militia commissioners because their unit had adopted prototype train-bands six years earlier, but their actions give us some idea of what happened elsewhere in the colony. They decided to muster their troops at four locations within the two sprawling counties: Charles City, Fort Henry, Flowerdew Hundred, and Rochdale Hundred. A typical proclamation announced that "all the freemen inhabiting in Henrico County, except Bristoll parish, shall meet and appear at a muster to be made at Roxdall on the 22th of this instant July about nine of the clock in the forenoone with their armes, and there give in their names, and lists of all their armes fixed and unfixed, servants and serviceable horses and mares, with account of theire severall ammunition, from which none to be exempted but Commissioners and sherifs, who notwithstanding are to send in their lists and accounts as aforesaid."[6]

The 1661 militia reform excluding unreliable servants from the trainbands seems to have led almost immediately to their exclusion from the general militia as well. At least that appears to have been the case in Henrico County, for the proclamation quoted above specifies that the Rochdale muster was for freemen only. At any rate, within a few years Virginians boasted that they could raise "20 Regiments of Foote, and as many troops of horse, without making use of any of our slaves, or fewe of our English servants."[7] No specific reason was given for this dramatic change in the makeup of the militia, but it probably was caused by increasing fear of servant revolt. If so, it was a timely act for the 1660s were marked by a number of abortive plots and uprisings. On the other hand, the exclusion of servants greatly decreased the pool of trained manpower in the colony and demolished the concept of the militia as the community in arms.

The troops that appeared at the Rochdale muster in Henrico County consisted of two companies of foot commanded by Major William Harris and Captain William Farrar and the new regimental

6. July 15, 1661, Charles City County Records, 1655/65, pp. 284–88.
7. Sir Henry Chicheley to Sir Thomas Chicheley, July 16, 1673, CO 1/30, f. 113.

troop of horse commanded by Captain Thomas Stagg. After the men had assembled and turned in the requisite information, which was duly forwarded to the governor, Harris and Farrar selected "a setled trained band" to protect the western frontier of Henrico County. This was one of the three small bands required of each regiment. When the band was complete, Major Harris exhorted its members "to be in continuall readinesse and preparation to march away with all possible speed" to the "allarme place at Captain Steggs plantation" near the falls of the James, from whence they would proceed to the endangered area. Miscellaneous announcements and other items of business followed, then the officers spent the afternoon exercising the troops. No doubt they were careful to follow Colonel Abraham Wood's orders to be "very wary and circumspect that no ammunition be spent and wast . . . but onely false fires to be given to prove the readinesse of their guns."[8]

The only significant organizational changes experienced by the Charles City–Henrico regiment in 1661 were the addition of dragoons and the creation of three small trainbands in place of the two original units. Besides the trainband near the falls of the James, a second band was established with a rendezvous point at Fort Henry, and a third was created on the south side with a rendezvous point at the head of Ward's Creek. All three designated gathering places were located on the outer fringes of settlement where an Indian incursion would most likely occur.[9] Other counties may have experienced more difficulty or been structured somewhat differently—without adequate records it is impossible to say—but it appears that by the end of the year all the provincial regiments had been remodeled more or less in accordance with Jamestown's grand design.

Thomas Ludwell, secretary of the colony, described the militia in 1666. At the apex of the command structure was the governor, Captain General Sir William Berkeley. He was assisted by his adjutant, Lieutenant General Sir Henry Chicheley, and assorted aides and guards. The colony was by this time divided into four military

8. July 15, 1661, Charles City County Records, 1655–65, pp. 284–88.
9. *Ibid.*

associations: lower James River, upper James River, York River, and Rappahannock River. Each association contained three to six counties. The upper James association was composed of "the next adjacent Counties to the Governor" and was "under his owne immediate Conduct." The other three associations, "being more remote," were commanded by three major generals and their adjutants. A fifth association, Potomac River, was created a few years later. Every county boasted trainbands, dragoons, and a "Regiment of Foot under the Command of a Collonell (who for the moste parte is one of the Councill) and other inferioure officers."[10] The militia had come of age. Unfortunately, Virginia's well-ordered paramilitary system would not long survive in this form. The associations, regiments, companies, troops, trainbands, and many other features would be gravely weakened or swept away by the force of Bacon's Rebellion.

But that was still well in the future, and Virginians at mid-century had several opportunities to put their evolving militia forces to the test. The 1650s and 1660s were years of rapid growth and expansion. Immigration increased around mid-century, and soon old and new planters were streaming up the broad tidewater rivers in search of suitable farmland. This movement inevitably provoked small, unsettling clashes with local Indians and brought the colonists into contact for the first time with the powerful "foreign" tribes of the interior. The postwar era began quietly enough. In 1651 Berkeley could state with obvious relief that "the Indians, God be blessed, round about us are subdued." But by November 1654 settlers in Lancaster, Northumberland, and Westmoreland counties, all new and located on the Northern Neck, were complaining of difficulties with the Rappahannock tribe. Jamestown responded by joining the three counties into a single military association, Rappahannock River, and suggesting that the new association handle its own problems. Taking the hint, a combined force of 170 northern troops marched to Rappahannock Town and cowed the inhabitants into a more submissive attitude.[11]

10. Thomas Ludwell to [Lord Arlington], September 17, 1666, CO 1/20, ff. 220–21.

11. Craven, *White, Red, and Black*, 58–62, and "Indian Policy," 76–82; Morgan, "Headrights and Head Counts," 361–71; "Speech of Sir William Berkeley, and Decla-

The next year was quiet, but in 1656 a more serious threat arose. Reports arrived in Jamestown that "many western and inland Indians are drawne from the mountaynes, and lately sett downe neer the falls of James river," perilously close to settlements in upper Henrico County. The Virginians were unsure of the identity or intentions of these intruders but assumed they were up to no good. Without bothering to learn more about the strangers, whom they called Ricahecrians, the colonists resolved that "these new come Indians be in noe sort suffered to seate themselves there, or any place near us[,] it haveing cost so much blood to expell and extirpate those perfidious and treacherous Indians which were there formerly, [and] It being so apt a place to invade us and within those lymitts which in a just warr were formerly conquered by us, and by us reserved at the last conclusion of peace with the Indians." The assembly authorized Colonel Edward Hill to raise one hundred men from his Charles City–Henrico regiment and remove the strange natives "without makeing warr if it may be" but by force of arms if necessary. In addition, the assembly called upon "all the neighbouring Indians" to assist the settlers in accordance with the mutual defense provisions of the 1646 treaty.[12]

Hill diligently set about "the raysing of a Considerable party of men" and convinced the chief of the Pamunkeys to lead a hundred or more of his warriors against the enemy in concert with the English. Topotomoi must have had mixed feelings about fighting alongside his new ally for he had recently complained to the governor that his brother had been killed by a settler. Nevertheless, in May or June the combined Anglo-Indian force moved upriver toward the strangers encamped near the falls. Hill then made a fatal mistake. Disobeying orders, he murdered five of the chiefs who came to parley with him. This act of "unparalleled hellish treachery" enraged the Ricahecrians, and somewhere near present-day Richmond, perhaps along the banks of a stream called Bloody Run, they defeated the Virginians. Details are scarce, but Topotomoi and many of his warriors were slain while the English troops fled to

---

ration of the Assembly, March 1651," *JHB*, I, 76; November 20, 1654, *Statutes*, I, 389–90.

12. March 10, 1655/6, *Statutes*, I, 402–403; April 23, June 5, 1656, *Minutes*, 504.

their boats and escaped down the river. Hill was condemned by unanimous vote of the council and assembly for his "crimes and weaknesses" during the disaster and temporarily suspended from all his civil and military offices.[13]

The defeat at Bloody Run is difficult to explain. The colonists apparently abandoned their Indian allies and the field before suffering any significant casualties. Their half of the expedition returned home embarrassingly intact while the Pamunkeys were butchered.[14] Why such a debacle? Possibly a battle was unexpected. The last full-scale engagement between English and Indian forces had occurred in 1624, more than thirty years earlier. For three decades colonial troops had wreaked havoc upon their enemies without actually participating in a pitched battle. The most recent march, for example, had cowed the Rappahannocks with only a show of force. The current generation of militiamen, familiar only with Indians who ran away from a fight, may have been unprepared for a stand-up battle. Or, because of the relatively rapid turnover among Virginia militiamen, a product of heavy immigration and low life expectancy, the expedition was burdened with too many green troops. If either of these suppositions is correct, a furious surprise assault launched upon the overconfident or inexperienced Englishmen probably would have been enough to send them reeling down the river.

Throughout the summer of 1656 the presence of these Indians greatly troubled the inhabitants of Charles City and Henrico counties. The region was swept by rumors of "suddaine Invasion," and local authorities prepared for the worst. But nothing happened. Sometime after Bloody Run the strange Indians at the falls disappeared as quietly and mysteriously as they had come.[15] This inglorious episode was a turning point of sorts for the militia. For the first time in recent memory the settlers had failed to overcome an

13. April 3, 1656, Charles City County Records, 1655–65, p. 44; Campbell, *History of the Colony*, 233–34; Washburn, *Virginia Under Charles I and Cromwell*, 54–55; June 7, 1655, *Minutes*, 503; December 1, 1656, *Statutes*, I, 422, 426.

14. The Charles City records list one wounded soldier. The only other colonial casualty seems to have been a horse. There is a passing reference to a "second Expedition" but nothing is known about this march (June 25, 1656, Charles City County Records, 1655–65, p. 54; December 1, 1656, *JHB*, I, 103).

15. July 25, 1656, Charles City County Records, 1655–65, p. 61.

Indian opponent—had, in fact, suffered a stinging tactical defeat. Bloody Run also was a warning of things to come. In the future Virginians would experience a great deal of harassment and worse from "foreign" or "northern" Indians based far beyond the colony's borders.

After two years of welcome peace and quiet, trouble developed in 1659 on the Eastern Shore. The Northampton County militia, reinforced by troops from York County, subdued the natives with little difficulty. About the same time problems arose once more on the Northern Neck. Several Englishmen in Northumberland County were murdered by renegades from local tribes. Indian leaders at first cooperated with local authorities by turning over some of the suspected murderers for trial and execution. But cooperation must have ceased shortly thereafter, for a column of Northumberland and Lancaster militiamen drove the Machoatick tribe from their village. When the natives began drifting back home the following spring, the Northumberland colonel dispatched another force to the Machoatick village to "burne their Cabins and cut up their Corne."[16]

By 1660 the method of reimbursing settlers for their military service was altered. The Charles City, Henrico, Northampton, York, and other county troops that had been called up during the past decade were paid in the manner established in 1624. Officers "strictly and exactly" calculated "the certaine time every soldier was out" and then informed all "those that stay at home" of the amount of work they owed the militiamen. The Northumberlanders called up in 1659 and apparently all militiamen in service after that date received a certain amount of tobacco from the county in lieu of having work done by neighbors. This change in policy may have been precipitated by the growing number of poor, landless colonists who could be effectively reimbursed only by a cash payment.[17] Unfortunately, this new policy meant that military service

16. November 13, 1660, October 1, 1661, York County Records, No. 3, Deeds, Orders, Wills, Etc., 1657–62, pp. 95–96, 136; May 6, August 6, November 23, 1659, May 3, 1660, Northumberland County Records, Order Book, 1652–65, pp. 110, 119, 122; November 30, 1659, Lancaster County Records, Orders, Etc., No. 3, 1655–66, p. 95.

17. November 13, 1660, York County Records, No. 3, Deeds, Orders, Wills, Etc., 1657–62, p. 95; November 23, 1659, Northumberland County Records, Order Book, 1652–65, p. 119; Morgan, *American Slavery*, 215–34.

and operations in the future would be more impersonal and more expensive.

Four years later the colony was rocked by the worst outbreak of Indian violence since the 1644 massacre. After several "horrid murthers" were committed, the assembly temporarily halted the establishment of new plantations unless they contained "fowre able hands well armed." Accounts of the incidents of 1664 are confusing and ambiguous. Southsiders reported that Tuscaroras from Carolina were "skulking about" and causing trouble. Westerners blamed the "treacherous mischiefes" on a nearby tribe. When a good part of the Charles City–Henrico regiment marched out on a punitive raid, relying on "secrecy from discovry and speedy endeavors" for the "surprisall" of the enemy, the records did not identify the object of the colonists' wrath.[18]

On the Northern Neck the colonists were beset by a small tribe called the Doegs, who lived some distance up the Potomac in Maryland. Major General Robert Smith, commander of the Potomac association, consulted Berkeley, who minced no words: "I thinke it is necessary to Distroy all these Northerne Indians," he wrote, and recommended that Smith's militiamen mount a campaign to smash the Doegs and any other hostiles in the vicinity. Such forceful action would be "a great Terror and Exemple of Instruction to all other Indians." He helpfully added that "if your young men will not Undertake it alone there will be enow [enough] from hence will undertake it for their Share of the Booty," meaning the selling of captive Indian women and children as slaves to the West Indies. The governor soon backed up his suggestions with an order from the council directing General Smith to see that the Doegs and their ilk "be forthwith persecuted with war to their utter destruction if possible."[19] But the proposed war of annihilation against

18. September 20, 1664, *Statutes*, II, 209; September 15, 1663, *JHB*, II, 23; October 19, 1664, November 10, 1665, Charles City County Records, 1655–65, pp. 513, 603–604.

19. September 10, 1663, *Statutes*, II, 193–94; May 27, 1664, Stafford County Records, Court Records, 1664–68, p. 1; December 21, 1666, Northumberland County Records, Order Book, 1666–78, p. 4; Berkeley to Major General Robert Smith, June 22, 1666, Rappahannock County Records, Deeds, Etc., No. 3, 1663–68, pp. 57–58; July 10, 1666, *Minutes*, 488–89.

the Doegs never took place. The order to march was canceled because the pacification of the northern frontier and Indian problems in general suddenly were overshadowed by alarming news from home. England and the Netherlands were at war, and the colonists hastened to put their coastal defenses in order.

The threat of invasion was nothing new in Virginia. Early settlers lived in constant fear of a Spanish attack, and the reason for locating Jamestown far upriver had been to make it less visible and vulnerable to an enemy naval force. In the summer of 1611 a lone Spanish caravel had sailed up to the lookout post on Point Comfort and brazenly demanded a pilot to take the ship upriver. The garrison naturally refused, but the caravel captured the only available pilot at the post and sailed away with him. Sir Thomas Dale, in command at the time, was understandably upset that the Spaniards now had "sufficiently instructed themselves concerning our just height and seate, and know the readie way unto us both by this discoverer, and by the help likewise of our owne Pilott." But there seemed little he or his men could do except await the enemy's next move.[20]

They did not have long to wait. Only a month later the shocking news reached Jamestown that a Spanish squadron had passed Point Comfort and was sailing up the James. Frenzied preparations were made to defend the little town. Dale "drewe All his forces into forme and order reddy for encownter" and polled his officers on whether to try to hold the fort or meet the enemy out on the river. George Percy favored the latter course, believing it "dowttfull whether our men wolde stande unto itt A shoare and Abyde the Brunte, butt A shippboard of necessety they muste for there was noe runneinge Away." Dale agreed with Percy and began loading his men aboard three ships riding before Jamestown. In a rousing speech he fired the settlers with the hope of victory if they readily obeyed his orders and assured them that if God willed their defeat, they could never fall in a more noble service. He concluded by pledging "to fire the Spanish Shippes with his owne" rather than surrender. Dale then manned a small boat with "thirty readie and

20. Dale to Lord Salisbury, August 17, 1611, *Genesis*, I, 507–508.

good shot" and dispatched them downriver to reconnoiter the invaders more closely. Fortunately, they found the "invaders" to be a fleet of five English supply ships, three of which were caravels transporting cattle. The edgy lookouts at Point Comfort had assumed they were Spanish. Strangely enough, despite considerable interest in the progress of the English colony, Spain made no attempt to eliminate it. Perhaps the settlement seemed too insignificant to destroy. Whatever the reason, the reconnaissance mission of 1611 was the sole Spanish appearance in Chesapeake Bay. The English, of course, had no way of knowing enemy intentions, and authorities in London and Jamestown remained preoccupied with the Spanish threat for another thirty years.[21]

Rumors of a Spanish assault in 1620–1621 were so convincing that Governor Yeardley attempted to strengthen the outpost at Point Comfort. It quickly became evident that Virginia had "no Engineers and arthmen to erect workes, few Ordenance, not a serviceable carriadge to mount them on; not Amunytion of powder, shott and leade, to fight 2 wholl dayes, no not one gunner belonging to the Plantation." Appalled, Yeardley asked London to send "choise men" from the Low Countries to design, construct, and garrison suitable coastal fortifications. The company declined to do so for financial reasons and suggested that the settlers make up in vigilance what they lacked in strength. Growing desperate, the Virginians then asked for a shipload of pikes, apparently convinced that their only hope of success was to repulse the invader at the water's edge. Such a prospect was not encouraging, and John Pory frankly admitted, "Hee that cann doe with a Pike is a better Soldier then I." Fortunately, although no pikes arrived, neither did the Spaniards.[22]

Despite the onset of the First Tidewater War in 1622 the English still felt it was "necessarie above all thinges, to secure the River from suddaine Invasion by Shipping." In the midst of a desperate

21. Percy, "Trewe Relacyon," 279; Hamor, *True Discourse*, 28–29; Andrews, *Colonial Period of American History*, I, 143–47; Wright, "Spanish Policy Toward Virginia," 448–79.

22. John Rolfe to Sir Edwin Sandys, January, 1619/20, *RVCL*, III, 244; George Thorpe and John Pory to Sir Edwin Sandys, May 15, 1621, *ibid.*, 447; Virginia Company to governor and council, December 5, 1621, *ibid.*, 530, 533.

struggle with the natives the Virginians attempted to erect a pair of small forts at Blunt Point and Wariscoyack, about halfway between Jamestown and Point Comfort. The two forts, facing each other across the river, were to be "intrenched about with deepe ditches" and equipped with "whole Culvering and demy-culvering at the least," if such "great ordnance" could be obtained from England. The work dragged on for more than a year, but the strain was too much for the sickly colony and the effort was abandoned early in 1624.[23]

Thus Virginia remained as "utterlye unfortified against a forren Enymie" as ever. One contemporary critic acidly remarked that the colony possessed "not the least peec of Fortification: Three peeces of Ordinance onely mounted att James Citty and one att Flowerdue hundred butt never a one of them serviceable; Soe that itt is most certaine that a Small Barke of 100 Tunn may take itts time to pass upp the River in spite of them; and comminge to an Anchor before the Towne may beat all their houses downe aboute their ears and soe forceinge them to retreat into the woods may Land under the favour of their Ordinance and rifle the Towne att pleasure." There was little argument about this dismal state of affairs. In 1627 the provincial government actually drew up a plan to evacuate and burn the settlements along the James should a Spanish flotilla enter that river. The colonists then would flee north across the peninsula and dig in on the bluffs above the York. The plan did not explain how the refugees would survive in the Indian-infested forests without food or shelter.[24]

This fatalistic attitude was swept away by the arrival of Governor Harvey, who quickly set about raising a fort of fourteen small guns at Point Comfort to replace the run-down lookout post. It is not known why the Virginians chose that particular spot or how they managed to obtain so many cannons, but in 1632 they in-

23. Virginia Company to governor and council, October 7, 1622, *ibid.*, 385; George Sandys to John Ferrar, April 8, 1623, *ibid.*, IV, 109; proclamation by Wyatt, April 29, 1623, *ibid.*, 129; warrants by Wyatt, May 13, November 20, December 8, 1623, *ibid.*, 191, 401, 441–42; council to commissioners, June 15, 1624, *ibid.*, 563–64.

24. Governor and council to commissioners, January 4, 1625/6, *ibid.*, IV, 568; Nathaniel Butler, "The Unmasked face of our Colony in Virginia as it was in the Winter of the yeare 1622," *ibid.*, II, 375; January 13, 1626/7, *Minutes*, 135–36.

formed London that the project "hath with incredible labour . . . and excessive chardge to the whole Colony beene brought to good perfection." The Virginians did not exaggerate; the cost of the fort was enormous. The project quintupled the rate of taxation and consumed about 80 percent of the colony's military budget in 1632, the final year of the First Tidewater War. In addition, the high cost of manning and maintaining the fort became an "insupportable burden." A permanent garrison of seven men—captain, gunner, drummer, and four crewmen—had to be paid, and the amateurish fort disintegrated faster than anyone expected. In 1640 extensive repairs were halted as "a vain and fruitless endeavor in regard of the apparent decay of the foundation," and yet another tax was levied to construct a new fortification and garrison house at the point. Little is known about this second fort except that it had a garrison of ten men and that it too fell into ruin.[25]

After these trials it is not surprising that interest in coastal fortifications declined during the next two decades. Spain was visibly weakening, and there now seemed little likelihood of an invasion from that quarter. Ironically, the only real threat at mid-century came when Virginia was briefly caught up in the turmoil of the English Civil War. In the spring of 1652 a parliamentary "fleete and force" arrived in Chesapeake Bay and demanded the surrender of the colony and its acknowledgment of the Commonwealth. Governor Berkeley assembled a large body of militia at Jamestown to oppose the landing, but cooler heads eventually prevailed. Berkeley temporarily stepped down and an honorable, almost amicable, capitulation was arranged so that "the ruine and destruction of the plantation" might be averted. The terms of surrender were mild. One article stipulated that all military equipment "other than for private use" had to be surrendered, but because nearly all weaponry in the colony was privately owned this probably had little effect on the militia.[26]

During the Interregnum England and the Netherlands became

25. Harvey to Privy Council, May 29, 1630, CO 1/5, f. 203; March 24, 1629/30, August 21, 1633, *Statutes*, I, 150, 222; March 6, 1631/2, *JHB*, I, 55; "Acts of the Generall Assembly," 145.

26. March 12, 1651/2, *Statutes*, I, 367–68, 365.

embroiled in a long struggle for dominance of maritime commerce in and around northern Europe. In 1664 the English capture of New Netherlands and other blatant acts of aggression triggered the second and most spectacular of the Anglo-Dutch wars.[27] This conflict, like the others, was fought almost entirely at sea, and it was clear that sooner or later the Dutch would turn their attention to the rich tobacco trade between the Chesapeake colonies and England. When Governor Berkeley, now restored to power, received word of the formal outbreak of hostilities in June, 1665, he hastened to put Virginia "into the best posture of defence the strength and situation of the place would permit." The derelict fort at Point Comfort erected in 1640 was ordered abandoned and the fourteen small guns there brought upriver to Jamestown. All merchant vessels in the colony were instructed to proceed to one of four places: Jamestown, Gloucester Point on the York, Corotoman Creek on the Rappahannock, and Pungoteague on the Eastern Shore. The ships were to ride "with ha[w]sers on the shore ready to hale on shore upon any approaching danger." As the merchantmen assembled, militiamen were sent to erect "a platform for battery and lines for small shott" at each of the four anchorages except Jamestown, where a somewhat more substantial fort was begun to hold most of the artillery from Point Comfort. Meanwhile, all regimental commanders were told to prepare the rest of their troops to "stand and remain ready to march" to the anchorages at the first alarm.[28]

Berkeley was cautiously optimistic. Without English men-of-war he could not prevent the Dutch from entering Chesapeake Bay, but perhaps the militia could frustrate the intruders. The governor estimated that he had about fifteen hundred "Dragooners" and twenty-five hundred "able men with snaphances" ready to fight and another three or four thousand poorly armed militiamen in reserve. Apparently he intended to use some of his men to hold the new fortifications, others to man the merchant vessels and repel would-be boarders, and the rest—presumably including all the horse-

27. Wilson, *Profit and Power*, 144–58; Geyl, *Netherlands in the Seventeenth Century*, 25–37, 85; Middleton, *Tobacco Coast*, 289–90.

28. Berkeley to the king, August 1, 1665, CO 1/9, f. 200; October 10, 1665, *Statutes*, II, 220–21; June 21, 1665, *Minutes*, 484–85.

men—to meet an enemy landing party. With these militiamen, wrote Berkeley, "I shal not doubt to encounter with as many strangers of what nation so ever they are when they are out of the protection of their Great Gunns which they can never manage halfe a mile within our thicke woods." Thomas Ludwell agreed. The Dutch "will burne our howses by the waters sides," he admitted candidly, "but wee shall undoubtedly make a longer march too dangerous for them unlesse their purchasse were greater then they can expect here." Fortunately for all concerned, the only Dutch fleet in American waters in 1665 passed up Chesapeake Bay in a vain attempt to recapture New Netherlands.[29]

The most damaging blow to strike Virginia at this time came from London rather than the Netherlands. When royal officials learned of Berkeley's decision to abandon Point Comfort, they insisted that the fortifications there be reconstructed and strengthened. Provincial authorities argued that experience had shown a fort at the point was "uselesse as to Any Certaintie of defence and insupporteable in the Charges of it . . . for the Entrance into the Province is soe large that any Enemy Shipp may ride out of all possible dainger of the greatest Cannon in the world." They begged to be allowed to continue work on the redoubts and the fort at Jamestown "in the Center and Hart of the Countrey" but to no avail. The king and Privy Council stood firm against this barrage of sound advice, and the Virginians reluctantly carried out their orders. The cannon at Jamestown were shipped back downriver, and hundreds of laborers, militiamen, and even sailors were pressed into service to "fill up the works with earth" on the barren peninsula. Work proceeded slowly, partly because of stormy weather and partly because of Berkeley's lack of confidence in the project, a fact clearly demonstrated in June, 1666, when a lone Dutch privateer slipped into the bay and captured two merchantmen. The governor's reaction was to order the workmen at the fort to bury the ordinance to prevent its capture by the enemy! After this fiasco,

29. Berkeley to [Richard Nicolls], June 21, 1665, July 30, 1666, BP; Berkeley to [Lord Arlington], August 1, 1665, CO 1/19, f. 202; Thomas Ludwell to [Lord Arlington], August 9, 1665, CO 1/19, f. 213; Geyl, *Netherlands in the Seventeenth Century*, 84–85.

further delays, the loss of several lives in construction accidents, and the expenditure of seventy thousand pounds of tobacco, the Virginians quietly halted work on the project. It had been another expensive failure.[30]

By the summer of 1667 the colony's coastal defenses were in a sorry state. The king had dispatched ten cannon for the better defense of Jamestown, but the other three redoubts remained empty and useless because all of Virginia's old artillery pieces were emplaced (or buried) in the unfinished earthworks at Point Comfort. Thus the strategists in London had sabotaged Berkeley's novel plan to protect the tobacco ships with the militia, though as we shall see, the general outlines of the plan were still in effect. The only bright spot was the recent arrival of the storm-damaged frigate *Elizabeth* in response to Jamestown's pleas for a naval force to seal off the entrance to Chesapeake Bay. While the *Elizabeth* was being refitted at Newport News and dozens of merchant vessels were gathering in the James and the York for the midsummer tobacco convoy to England, the war suddenly heated up. At almost the same time the main Dutch fleet under Admiral Michel A. de Ruyter was making its spectacular raid on the Medway near London, a small Dutch flotilla was approaching the Virginia capes.[31]

Admiral Abraham Crijnsen (or Crimson as the colonists called him) had recently captured Surinam from the English and was cruising up the North American coast looking for trouble. His squadron of four men-of-war of thirty-eight, thirty-four, twenty-four, and eighteen guns and a "Dogger Boate" of eight guns arrived off the entrance to Chesapeake Bay on June 1 and seized a merchantman and a small coasting vessel. Upon learning from his captives of the promising situation in Virginia, Crijnsen quietly slipped into the Chesapeake and spent several days preparing for battle.

30. March 29, July 10, 1666, *Minutes*, 487–88; governor and council to Lord Arlington, July 13, 1666, CO 1/20, f. 199; November 8, 1666, *JHB*, II, 42; Thomas Ludwell to Lord Arlington, February 12, 1666/7, CO 1/21, f. 38.

31. Governor and council to king and Privy Council [June, 1667], CO 1/21, ff. 109–12; Thomas Ludwell to [Lord Arlington], June 24, 1667, CO 1/21, ff. 113–14; "Attacks by the Dutch on the Virginia fleet," 229–45. The ten cannons sent to Jamestown were two culverins, two demiculverins, and six sakers ("An Account of Ordnance and other Stores of War Sent to the Plantations, 1660–1688," February 11, 1700, CO 323/4).

On June 5 his warships raised English flags and cautiously followed the captured shallop past Point Comfort and up the unfamiliar channel of the James, the crews loudly chanting soundings and hailing other ships in English. A few miles upriver the *Elizabeth* lay at anchor, her unsuspecting captain ashore "with his wench that he carryed with him from England" along with most of the other officers and crew. The Dutch men-of-war crept up on the frigate, suddenly fired several shattering broadsides, and closed to board. The astounded English skeleton crew returned a single shot and then abandoned ship to the enemy. The Dutch were unable to make a prize of the frigate for her sails and rigging had been taken ashore for repairs, so they burned her on the spot. Few if any of the nearby merchant vessels attempted to escape during the brief battle; most remained at anchor and surrendered when the Dutch approached. By the end of the day Admiral Crijnsen was master of the lower James.[32]

When Berkeley learned what was happening downriver he "resolved to man out a fleet from Yorke river being nearest to the enimy and hasten to them and fight them." It was a plan born of desperation. The Dutch had destroyed the lone English warship in the area and were threatening the many merchantmen trapped upriver at Jamestown. The only hope of saving that part of the tobacco fleet (and perhaps Jamestown as well) was to attack the Dutch ships from above and below in the relatively narrow confines of the James River, close with them, and overwhelm them with superior numbers of men. The Virginians had no choice but to take the offensive. To this end Berkeley quickly assembled three "regiments of foot"—about nine hundred militiamen—and packed them and the crew of the *Elizabeth* aboard the nine largest merchant vessels riding in the York River. He then piled on board so many cannon from smaller vessels that his nine ships were more heavily armed than their Dutch adversaries. The three largest merchantmen at Jamestown were fitted out in similar fashion and manned with a fourth infantry regiment. At the appropriate time, while the

32. Blok, *History of the People of the Netherlands*, IV, 338; governor and council to king and Privy Council [June, 1667], ff. 109–10; Ludwell to [Arlington], June 24, 1667; memo of the merchant of the *Handmaid* [June, 1667], CO 1/21, f. 115.

York merchantmen rounded the peninsula and slowly made their way upriver toward the enemy squadron, these vessels at the capital would drop down the James and take them in the rear. When all seemed in readiness the elderly governor boarded the largest ship in the "Yorke fleet" and declared his determination to lead them to victory or die in the attempt. With him went nearly fifty gentleman-planter-officers and the mortified captain of the *Elizabeth,* who for obvious reasons was "very passionately resolved to hazard himself in the Admirall [flagship] with the Governor and the rest of his Company." The Virginia militia (with a little help) was about to fight its first naval battle.[33]

Alas, nothing happened. Despite Governor Berkeley's desire to raise anchor and get on with the battle, "every hower new difficulties" were raised by the reluctant merchant captains, whose initial zeal for this daring enterprise had faded considerably. In the beginning, wrote Ludwell, the captains had loudly proclaimed their intentions of fighting the Dutch, "yet when they saw it would come to earnest they grew very cold" and managed to delay the assault until it was too late. After five days Admiral Crijnsen decided his men and ships had done as much damage as they could. He also may have been aware that the Virginians were prepared to fight. He placed prize crews aboard a dozen or more captured tobacco ships, burned five or six others, and sailed away in triumph. The "Crimson Raid" was over.[34]

The Dutch victory was humiliating but hardly disastrous. Most of the tobacco fleet had survived, and the militia had faced the crisis well. As Berkeley and Ludwell had predicted, the Virginians won several sharp skirmishes with enemy landing parties in search of plunder and provisions. Major General Richard Bennett, commander of the lower James association, in particular, "behaved himself very bravely in defence of the shore" in Elizabeth City County. During the entire affair the colonial troops ashore and aboard ship reportedly "expressed as much cheerfullness in their Countries service and as much affection to theire Generall as ever men

33. Ludwell to [Arlington], June 24, 1667; governor and council to king and Privy Council [June, 1667].

34. *Ibid.*

did," in marked contrast to the shameful behavior of some of the merchant captains.[35]

Far more damaging than the Dutch raiders was a "Dreadfull Hurry Cane" that devastated the hapless colony in late August. The storm had one positive effect, however, for it washed away the works at Point Comfort and temporarily settled the argument over the best method of coastal defense. The Virginians now were free to continue fortifying Jamestown and the mouths of the four major rivers. At great expense they strengthened the fort at the capital, enlarged the redoubts at Gloucester Point and Corotoman Creek, and erected two new ones at Nansemond and at Yocomico on the Potomac. (Apparently the redoubt at Pungoteague on the Eastern Shore was abandoned.) Each of these five substantial structures was designed to hold "eight greate guns at the least," have walls ten feet high and ten feet thick, and contain "a court of guard and a convenient place to preserve the magazine." The settlers hoped to "Apparell" these forts with heavy cannon from the sunken *Elizabeth* but found that the guns were unserviceable. They appealed to the king without success for forty to fifty culverin and demiculverin. By the end of the decade the colonists were more impoverished than ever, and the colony remained almost completely open to attack from the sea.[36]

The outbreak of the third and final Anglo-Dutch war in 1672 caused worried provincial officials to review once again the state of the colony's defenses. They found that the weapons shortage had, if anything, worsened. In April, 1673, the governor and council ordered all militia officers to muster their troops "and take Care that what Armes shall bee in any Howse more then the people Listed Can use be secured for those who shall be found wanting of Armes." All guns, powder, and shot found in stores and warehouses also were requisitioned and distributed among needy militiamen. But there was not enough military equipment in Virginia to go around. A few months later the assembly authorized militia com-

35. *Ibid.*
36. Thomas Ludwell to Lord Berkeley, November 7, 1667, CO 1/21, f. 282; Berkeley to [Lord Arlington], November 11, 1667, *ibid.*, p. 286; September 23, 1667, *Statutes*, II, 255–59; Thomas Ludwell to [Lord Arlington], July 20, 1668, June 7, 1669, CO 1/23, f. 31, CO 1/24, f. 118.

missioners in each county to purchase arms and ammunition abroad, the first major public expenditures for small arms since 1640. Sketchy, incomplete records indicate that some commissioners ignored the assembly's instructions. More than two years later four companies of the Middlesex regiment were found to be in need of two hundred firearms and an equal number of swords and bandoliers. Other commissioners were more conscientious. York County spent sixty-one thousand pounds of tobacco in 1674–1675 for "such Armes as are found wanting (vizt) for the Troope [of horse] Seaventy Cuttlases with wast belts, fiftie Carbines and belts, fortie Case of pistolls and Holsters with breast plates and Cruppers; for Colonel Bacons regiment Eighty Musketts firelocks and one hundred and sixty Swords and belts; for Colonel Beales regiment seaventy Musketts firelocks and Seaventy Cutlases with wast belts and amunition." These new weapons were generally stored in the homes or barns of prominent county officials and loaned to militiamen going on active duty. It is not known how many weapons were ordered altogether or whether their arrival significantly alleviated the overall shortage. Most of this equipment arrived from England too late to be of use in the Dutch wars but just in time for Bacon's Rebellion.[37]

The expensive and largely empty coastal fortifications, though less than five years old, had been poorly built, and the earthworks were eroding faster than they could be repaired. It was a familiar story, and Berkeley, like Wyatt and Harvey before him, explained to his superiors in London: "We have neither skill or ability to make or mainetaine [our fortifications] for there is not now as farr as my inquiry ran [or] ever was one Ingeneir in the Country soe that wee are at continuall charge to repaire unskillfull and inartificiall buildings of that nature."[38]

Despite the shortage of arms and the crumbling forts, Berkeley

37. Governor and assembly to [Thomas Chicheley], September 24, 1672, *JHB*, II, 58–59; Berkeley to [Lords Commissioners for Trade and Plantations], March 25, 1673, CO 1/30, f. 41; April 22, 1673, *Minutes*, 334; October 20, 1673, *Statutes*, II, 304–305; May 25, 1674, October 26, 1675, York County Records, No. 5, Deeds, Orders, Wills, Etc., 1672–76, pp. 68, 129; May 1, 1676, Middlesex County Records, Order Book, 1673–80, f. 58.

38. "An Answer to the Inquiries of the . . . Lords Commissioners for Forreigne Plantations," June 20, 1671, CO 1/26, f. 197.

was determined to prevent another humiliating enemy triumph in Virginia. The militia was readied once again to march to the defense of the tobacco fleet. Painfully aware that the Dutch "may come on the Soddaine and Attacque the shipps within our Harbours," the governor and council ordered militia officers near the mouths of the rivers "upon the First allarme" to put aboard each merchant vessel fifty well-armed men "to serve as smale shott to defend the said shipp." Perhaps these were trainbands. The remainder of the twenty regiments of foot and twenty troops of horse were to take up positions in the forts and along the banks of the rivers as quickly as possible. Virginia's leaders were considerably less confident than they had been eight years earlier. Although they had done well enough in their last encounter with the Dutch, Berkeley fretted that many of his troops were "unacquainted with dainger" and questioned their "Courage against an Enemy better practiced in the Hazards of Warr." Sir Henry Chicheley was even more pessimistic. He feared the colonists would "be forced to fly to the mountains for our security, and leave this Country and our estates a prey to the invaders." The arrival in June, 1673, of two English frigates probably lifted their sagging spirits a bit.[39]

The timely appearance of the royal navy saved the day. On July 11 came the dreaded news that a flotilla of nine Dutch warships had passed the capes and was approaching the mouth of the James. Captains Jacob Bincks and Cornelius Everson were not so lucky as Admiral Crijnsen, however, for this time the English were forewarned and the intruders soon found themselves entangled in a wild melee in Hampton Roads. While Berkeley mobilized the militia, the two English frigates and six heavily armed merchantmen sallied forth from Newport News to engage the enemy. This hasty attack was made to prevent the Dutch from capturing a group of unsuspecting Maryland tobacco ships coming in to join the midsummer convoy to England. In the confused battle that followed, one Marylander and four of the armed merchantmen went aground and were lost, but the remaining English vessels put up a terrific

39. April 22, 1673, *Minutes*, 334; October 20, 1673, *Statutes*, II, 304–305; governor and council to the king [July 16, 1673], CO 1/30, ff. 114–15; Sir Henry Chicheley to Sir Thomas Chicheley, July 16, 1673, CO 1/30, f. 113.

fight against the entire Dutch squadron before withdrawing safely into the Elizabeth River. Meanwhile, nearly two dozen other vessels retreated to the security of Jamestown and another dozen or so gathered under the eroding ramparts of Nansemond fort. At the latter place the Netherlanders "looked on them five Dayes but Attempted them not," unaware that the fort contained nothing more powerful than a company of southside infantry. Frustrated by the frigates and forts, Bincks and Everson destroyed a half-dozen more grounded merchantmen in Virginia's waters and then departed for New York, which they recaptured briefly for the Netherlands. Thus ended the third and last Dutch raid on Virginia.[40]

The militia played only a minor role in this encounter. The troops boarded merchant vessels, occupied the forts, and patrolled the shoreline as planned but apparently did not attempt to engage the enemy. Their lack of involvement may have been fortunate, for a strange malaise had settled over the colony. The freemen who made up the vast bulk of the militia were as demoralized as their leaders; gone was the "cheerfullness" remarked upon six years earlier. Many of the troops—established planters and frontiersmen—were worried about servant unrest and recent Indian depredations. "It Troubled them much to be drawne away from their Worke (though for their Common defense)," wrote Berkeley, for "Wee leave at our backs as Many Servants (besides Negroes) as their are freemen to defend the Shoars and all our Fronteirs [against] the Indians, Both which gives men fearfull apprehentions of the dainger they Leave their Estates and Families in, Whilest they are drawne from their houses to defend the Borders." Many other troops—young, landless, and impoverished freemen—were dangerously close to revolt themselves. After the Dutch withdrawal Berkeley quickly ordered the unhappy and restless militiamen back to their homes. He then hastened about the colony, "visiting the remoter parts, and with his presence encouraging every one to bee well in their places." The personal popularity of the old governor temporarily appeased the discontent.[41]

40. Governor and council to the king [July 16, 1673].

41. *Ibid.*; council to the king and Privy Council [July, 1673], CO 1/30, f. 179; Morgan, *American Slavery*, 215–34.

By the 1670s the Virginia militia had become a troubled institution, unavoidably affected by the colony's rapidly mounting social, economic, and political problems. Half the male population had been excluded from the militia, but many of those still within the provincial forces were ill-armed, unhappy, unreliable, or potentially rebellious. The militia's increasingly sophisticated form could neither mask these problems nor prevent them from tearing the institution apart in the upheaval to come.

6. Bacon's Rebellion

The end of the Dutch wars brought little peace to Virginia. In July, 1675, a party of Doegs murdered a settler and a friendly Indian on an isolated farm in the extreme northern part of the colony. Upon discovery of the bodies, Colonel George Mason and Major George Brent of the Stafford County militia assembled the local trainband and set out after the Doegs. The trail led across the Potomac River into Maryland, where the Virginians caught up with the raiding party and killed eleven of them. Unfortunately, in the confusion the militiamen also killed fourteen Susquehannock Indians a short distance away. The unprovoked attack enraged the Susquehannocks, and during the next few weeks they retaliated with murderous forays against frontier settlements in Virginia and Maryland. The Susquehannock War and the tragic series of events leading to Bacon's Rebellion were under way.[1]

Reports arriving in Jamestown from distant Stafford County were so confusing the governor and council directed two Westmoreland County officers, Colonel John Washington and Major Isaac Allerton, to make "a full And thorough inquisittion" into the entire affair and determine exactly what had happened and which tribes were responsible for the current outrages. Upon completing this investigation the two officers were to take whatever action they deemed necessary, including the raising of "a fitt number of men" from the two northern associations to march against the guilty Indians. Washington and Allerton decided not to conduct an investigation. Instead, they wrote to the governor of Maryland and proposed a joint campaign against the Doegs and Susquehannocks. Because the operation would take place within Maryland, Major Thomas Truman of that colony was appointed overall commander.

1. Sir John Berry and Francis Moryson, "A True Narrative of the Late Rebellion in Virginia, by the Royal Commissioners, 1677," and [Thomas Mathew], "The Beginning, Progress, and Conclusion of Bacon's Rebellion, 1675–1676," *Narratives*, 105–106, 16–18; August 31, 1675, Westmoreland County Records, Deeds, Patents, Etc., 1665–77, f. 232. Throughout this chapter I have relied principally on Morgan, *American Slavery*, and, to a lesser extent, on Washburn, *Governor and the Rebel*, and Wertenbaker, *Torchbearer of the Revolution*.

About five hundred Virginians and half that number of Marylanders, both horse and foot, were called up for the expedition.[2]

The two columns rendezvoused on September 26 at the juncture of the Potomac River and Piscataway Creek in Maryland (roughly opposite Mount Vernon). The Doegs had dispersed, but the Susquehannocks were crowded into a two-hundred-foot-square fort that had been erected by Maryland in 1642 as a frontier outpost and then abandoned. Now, strengthened and manned by a hundred Indian warriors, it was a formidable defensive position. According to planter Thomas Mathew:

> The Walls of this fort were high banks of Earth, with Flankers having many Loop Holes, and a Ditch round all, and without this a Row of Tall Trees fastned 3 foot Deep in the Earth, their Bodies from 5 to 8 Inches Diameter, watled 6 Inches apart to shoot through with the Tops twisted together, and also Artificially Wrought, as our Men [i.e., and all so artfully wrought that our men] could make no Breach to Storm it, nor (being Low Land) coud they undermine it by reason of Water—neither had they Cannon to batter itt, So that 'twas not taken, untill Famine drove the Indians out of it.

The colonists had no choice but to lay siege to the fort. When the Susquehannocks realized the troops intended to stay, five of their chiefs came out to parley but were killed on Major Truman's orders. After this senseless act of treachery, the Indians resisted furiously, "making frequent, fierce and Bloody Sallyes" against the colonists "who kep such neglegent gards, that there was very few days past without som remarkeable mischeife." About fifty militiamen were killed or wounded in these forays, demonstrating the lack of discipline and professionalism inherent in the militia. The siege ended abruptly after seven weeks when the Susquehannocks burst out of the fort one night and swept through the English lines to freedom, killing another ten besiegers on the way. The disheartened Virginians and Marylanders made no attempt to pursue. They

2. August 31, 1675, Westmoreland County Records, Deeds, Patents, Etc., 1665–77, f. 232; John Washington and Isaac Allerton to governor and council of Maryland, September 6, 1675, and governor and council of Maryland to Washington and Allerton, September 14, 1675, *Archives*, XV, 48–49.

burned the fort, parted company, and returned home. The joint expedition had been an expensive and demoralizing failure.[3]

Worse was to come. During the next few months the Susquehannocks gained their revenge by ravaging Virginia's northwestern frontier. The worst blow fell on the isolated farmsteads along the upper Rappahannock River, where, on January 25, 1676, thirty-six people were killed in a single Indian raid. As news spread of this and other murderous assaults, a terrible fear gripped the outermost settlements. One colonist recalled:

> In these frightfull times the most Exposed small families withdrew into our houses of better Numbers, which we fortified with Pallisadoes and redoubts, Neighbours in Bodies Joined their Labours from each Plantation to others Alternately, taking their Arms into the Fields, and Setting Centinels; no Man Stirrd out of Door unarm'd, Indians were (ever and anon) espied, Three, 4, 5, or 6 in a Party Lurking throughout the Whole Land, yet (what was remarkable) I rarely heard of any Houses Burnt, tho' abundance was forsaken, nor ever, of any Corn or Tobacco cut up, or other Injury done, besides Murders, Except the killing [of] a very few Cattle and Swine.

The Susquehannocks cut a swath through the frontier counties, moving roughly from north to south down the fall line. They seemed uninterested in spoil or plunder or in driving the English away; they wanted only revenge and a steady supply of food. After a month or two of mayhem they were satisfied. Having avenged the murder of their chiefs, they offered to make peace with the Virginians. Berkeley naturally rejected the proposal. Rebuffed, the Susquehannocks gradually withdrew to the south and west.[4]

Their departure did little to relieve the situation. An assortment of marauders picked up where the Susquehannocks left off. Some

3. The expedition was, if nothing else, a remarkable exercise in logistics. The two colonies apparently kept most of the men in the field for two months. See Ferguson, "Susquehannock Fort," 1–9; "The History of Bacon's and Ingram's Rebellion, 1676," *Narratives*, 47–48, 19, 106; testimony of John Gerrard, Westmoreland County Records, Deeds, Patents, Etc., 1665–77, f. 288; May 19–June 1, 1676, *Archives*, II, 481–501.

4. Grievances of Sittingbourne Parish, Rappahannock County, March 8, 1676/7, CO 1/39, f. 200; *Narratives*, 19–20, 48–50; Berkeley to [?], April 1, 1676, CO 1/36, f. 66.

were foreign or northern Indians of uncertain identity; others were more familiar. Contemporary accounts agree that most subject tribes, that is, those Indians who had submitted to English authority since 1646, remained loyal or at least neutral in 1676 and even fought alongside the English on occasion. But these same accounts also agree that a substantial number of tidewater Indians defected and did great damage because of their intimate knowledge of terrain, settlements, and English habits. The colonists may have been largely to blame for this calamitous turn of events. Robert Beverley stated that the fury of the Susquehannock raids caused many frontiersmen to panic and conclude that a general insurrection of the subject tribes was in progress. These tribes soon noticed what Beverley quaintly termed "an unusual Uneasiness in the English, and being terrified by their rough Usage, immediately suspected some wicked Design against their Lives, and so fled to their remoter Habitations. This confirm'd the English in the Belief, that they had been the Murderers, till at last they provoked them to be so in Earnest."[5]

Now the character of the assaults began to change. Cornfields were razed, herds slaughtered, and abandoned houses and barns put to the torch. Organization and communications broke down among the scattered groups huddled together for protection. Maintaining an adequate defense was difficult enough under these circumstances; carrying out effective offensive operations was practically impossible. Help from counties behind the front was desperately needed, and urgent appeals for arms, ammunition, and, above all, reinforcements were hurried to Jamestown. At first Berkeley responded with his usual aggressiveness. Bypassing the association structure, he ordered his principal lieutenant, Sir Henry Chicheley, to take a strong force of horse and foot up the Rappahannock and relieve the hard-pressed settlers in that area. Then, suddenly, inexplicably, he canceled the order, disbanded the troops, and re-

5. *Narratives*, 49–50; Beverley, *History and Present State of Virginia*, 77; governor and assembly to the king, June 25, 1676, CO 1/37, f. 33. The outbreak of King Philip's War in New England at almost exactly the same time made the Virginians even more convinced of an Indian conspiracy (Washburn, "Governor Berkeley and King Philip's War," 363–77).

ferred the matter to the next assembly as if it were a routine piece of business![6]

Berkeley's incredible turnabout stunned the colony. Residents of Rappahannock County, who had heard that help finally was on the way, were bitterly disappointed. They condemned the governor's sudden inertia "whilest poore Rappahannock lies a bleeding" and castigated their fellow Virginians (a bit unfairly) for being "soe narrow hearted and close fisted as to think it none of their duty to assist us in destroying the blood thirsty Indians, but would willingly leave us to fight the battles of the Republique." Similar outraged protests were heard from other western counties, but Berkeley ignored them all. By the time the assembly finally met in March, "neer 300 Christian persons" had been killed by Indians, many of them after hideous tortures. The country was in an uproar.[7]

At the meeting of the assembly the legislators were dominated by the aging governor and did his bidding. They decided against a "Flying army" and established a passive, fixed-point defense wholly unsuited to the task at hand. They ordered a string of nine palisaded forts erected all around the colony. A construction and garrison force of five hundred militiamen (a fourth of them dragoons) was raised from "the midland and most secure parts of the country," which included all but Stafford, Westmoreland, Rappahannock, and Henrico counties. The dragoons were expected "to range constantly betweene the garrisons" in search of Indian raiding parties moving toward the settlements. A few reliable Indians were assigned to each fort as scouts for these "rangers." The remaining militia forces in adjacent counties were supposed to stand ready to "march to the reliefe of the Forts" or act in concert with their garrisons as required. Cooperation among the various units was emphasized; initiative was not. After the blunders in Maryland the assembly insisted that the discovery of an enemy camp or force be reported to Jamestown at once and that "noe attempt be made upon

6. Grievances of Blissland Parish, New Kent County, April 4, 1677, CO 1/39, f. 233; *Narratives*, 107.

7. Grievances of Rappahannock County, March 13, 1676/7, CO 1/39, f. 197; *Narratives*, 50, 107–108.

them by any comander whatsoever untill order shall come from the governour."[8]

This plan may have looked good on paper in Jamestown, but it met with "the universal dislike of the People throughout the Countrey, And accordingly was Laid aside, or at most very slowly prosecuted." The plan had several drawbacks. It was expensive. The public was expected to provide the troops with fixed salaries and all necessary implements and provisions for an indefinite period. Food alone came to ten thousand pounds of meat and more than seven hundred bushels of corn per month. Worse, the plan was passive and tactically unsound. It seemed designed to protect the forts instead of the frontier population. The six or seven forts that were erected failed to prevent incursions by an aggressive and resourceful enemy. According to one settler, "The Indians quickly found out where about these Mouse traps were sett, and for what purpose, and so resalved to keepe out of there danger; which they might easely ennough do, with out any detriment to there designes." Finally, the order forbidding attacks on Indians without the governor's permission was wholly impractical. Discontent flamed into anger as Indian attacks continued without letup. Under this terrible strain Virginia's political and social fabric began to weaken.[9]

The breakdown began in the paramilitary system. In late March the long-suffering residents of Charles City and Henrico counties learned (incorrectly as it turned out) that "Several formidable Bodies of Indians" were moving downriver in their direction. Terrified at this "approaching calamity," the local militia resolved to meet the enemy above the falls of the James in a desperate attempt to protect their farms and families. The troops repeatedly petitioned the governor for permission to march. They even offered to bear their own expenses in defense of their homes—a rare sentiment in late seventeenth-century Virginia. Berkeley rejected their petitions and warned them not to send him any more. The governor had made a fatal error. His refusal "made the giddy-headed multitude madd, and precipitated them upon that rash overture of Running

8. March 7, 1675/6, *Statutes*, II, 326–40.

9. *Ibid.*, 329–40; governor and assembly to the king, June 25, 1676; *Narratives*, 50–51, 108; February 20, 1676/7, *JHB*, II, 84–85; grievances of Henrico County, March

out upon the Indians themselves, at their owne voluntary charge and hazard of their Lives and Fortunes."[10] The spark had been lighted that set off Bacon's Rebellion.

Events of the next few months are familiar to most students of Virginia history. The angry militiamen "wanted nor waited for nothing but one to head and lead them out on their design." A councillor and Henrico planter named Nathaniel Bacon, Jr., soon appeared on the scene and supplied the necessary leadership and authority, though he had no military rank. With Bacon at their head the insurgents attracted a large number of like-minded volunteers from adjacent New Kent County and set out to smite the savages. Berkeley promptly proclaimed them rebels and led a party of dragoons up the James "to call Mr. Bacon to accompt." But the old man was too late. The rebel councillor and his "rabble Crue" already had gone.[11]

Bacon's little army failed to find any threatening body of Indians above the falls and wandered aimlessly off to the southwest. After several days the English reached the territory of the Occaneechee tribe, a foreign but friendly people who lived on a fortified island in the Roanoke River a few miles below present-day Clarksville. The Occaneechees informed Bacon that a small band of Susquehannocks was camped nearby. He asked them to attack the Susquehannocks, which they did with great success, bringing in prisoners and a pile of beaver pelts. At this point the English and their hosts began to quarrel, probably over the furs, and a fierce battle broke out on the crowded island. The soldiers fired first and killed or captured about fifty Occaneechees, mainly women and children. They hastily withdrew the next day, leaving behind a dozen or more of their own dead. Bacon returned from this adventure "with a thousand braging lyes to the credulous Silly People of what feats

16, 1676/7, CO 1/39, f. 238; grievances of Charles City County, May 10, 1677, CO 1/40, f. 142.

10. *Narratives*, 51–53, 108–109; Berkeley to the king, March 24, 1676, CP, LXXVII, 66; petition to Berkeley from "your poore distressed Subjects in the upper parts of James River in Virginia" [March or April, 1676], CO 1/36, f. 139.

11. *Narratives*, 21, 52–53, 109–12; Morgan, *American Slavery*, 254–59; [William Sherwood], "Virginias Deploured Condition: Or an Impartiall Narrative of the Murders comitted by the Indians there," *Collections*, 167; declaration by Berkeley, May 10, 1676, CO 1/37, f. 2.

he had perform'd," boasting that his troops "Storm'd and burnt the Fort and Cabins, and (with the Losse of Three English) Slew 150 Indians." He need not have exaggerated his accomplishments. The simple fact that he had acted and had killed Indians—any Indians—made him a hero.[12]

Berkeley, meanwhile, finally realized that the frontier counties were dangerously close to revolt because of his passive conduct of the war. He hurried back to Jamestown and called another assembly, whereupon the people of Henrico County impudently selected Bacon as one of their delegates to the House of Burgesses. Upon approaching the capital, Bacon was arrested and brought before the governor. He quickly admitted the error of his ways and was pardoned and reinstated on the council. The affair might have ended there but for the behavior of Bacon's followers. When news of his arrest reached the southwestern frontier, an "abundance of Men" set out at once for Jamestown to free him. The marching columns turned back only upon learning of Bacon's release and restoration to the council. After this unexpected show of support the councillor began to regret his premature capitulation and soon slipped out of town.[13]

A few days later news came that Bacon and five hundred men were approaching Jamestown. Berkeley summoned the nearby James City and York trainbands to defend the capital, but his summons was largely ignored. He then attempted to mount four cannons from the fort in a "Barracadoe" across the narrow neck of land connecting Jamestown to the main. Work was proceeding very slowly when suddenly "the cry was Armes, Armes, Bacon is within two Myles of the Towne." Realizing the hopelessness of the situation, Berkeley had the cannon dismounted and retired to the statehouse to await his antagonist. On the afternoon of June 23, 1676, Bacon and

12. *Narratives*, 21, 113, 123; [Sherwood], "Virginias Deploured Condition," *Collections*, 167–68; "A Discription of the Fight between the English and the Indians in Virginia in May 1676," CO 1/36, ff. 211–12; Abraham Wood to Berkeley, May 24, 1676, CP, LXXVII, p. 88; Philip Ludwell to [Sir Henry Coventry], June 28, 1676, CO 1/37, f. 36; Washburn, ed., "Sir William Berkeley's 'A History of Our Miseries,'" 406–408, and *Governor and the Rebel*, 42–46.

13. *Narratives*, 21–28, 54–55, 113–16; Philip Ludwell to [Lady Frances Berkeley], June 12, 1676, CP, LXXVII, p. 117; Washburn, *Governor and the Rebel*, 49–56.

his militiamen entered Jamestown "without being withstood, and form'd a Body upon a green, not a flight Shot from the End of the Statehouse, of Horse and Foot, as well regular as Veteran troops." They disarmed everyone in the town and posted guards in the fort, on the neck of land, and at the ferry landing. The capital and government of Virginia were in their hands.[14]

Berkeley and his faithful few often denounced the insurgents as "rabble," "the meanest sort of people," and "the scume of the Country," but these labels are misleading. All of Bacon's followers at this point were frontier militiamen—in some cases entire militia units complete with officers. Observers noted that the insurgents were "good Howsekeepers, well armed," who marched and drilled "as well regular as Veteran troops" and generally carried on "in a military posture." By and large, they were the younger, poorer freemen who tended to settle along the frontier and were motivated to protest because Virginia's political institutions had failed to cope with their growing anger and frustration.[15] The militia provided them with organization, a sense of common purpose, a certain degree of autonomy, and regular opportunities to meet and talk. Under the circumstances it was hardly surprising that the militia should become the vehicle of protest and, soon, rebellion.

But rebellion was not yet their purpose. Bacon had not led his small army to Jamestown to depose Berkeley or topple the government but to demand permission to move against the Indians. By this time the June assembly had drawn up a more aggressive plan for carrying on the war. The unpopular forts at the falls of the rivers were to be abandoned and their garrisons "quartered and disposed in the fronteere plantations" nearby. A thousand additional militiamen were to be raised to carry the war to the enemy. This force was to be divided into two armies of roughly equal strength: a southern column composed of men from the two James River associations (plus York County) and a northern column composed of

14. *Narratives*, 28, 55; William Sherwood to [?], June 28, 1676, CO 1/37, f. 39; Philip Ludwell to [?], June 28, 1676, CO 1/37, f. 37.

15. [Sherwood], "Virginias Deploured Condition," *Collections*, 171, 166; governor and council to commissioners for trade and plantations, May 31, 1676, CP, LXXVII, pp. 95–96; Philip Ludwell to [?], June 28, 1676, CO 1/37, f. 35; *Narratives*, 28, 55, 116; Morgan, *American Slavery*, 265; Kelly, "In dispers'd Country Plantations," 183–205.

men from the York, Rappahannock, and Potomac river associations. Every soldier was to carry a gun, two pounds of powder, and six pounds of shot and to be supplied with "one pound of biscake bread, and one halfe pound of good dried beefe, bacon or cheese" per day. Each of the "marching armies" was to include two surgeons and sixty pack animals. Officers and men were to be exempt from taxes for a year and paid regular wages in tobacco by both their counties and the provincial government. Subject Indians were to be recruited as scouts and warriors wherever possible. The assembly also dashed off an urgent request to the king for enough weaponry to equip a thousand infantrymen and six hundred horsemen.[16]

Virginia would have fielded the largest and costliest expedition in its brief history if this ambitious plan had been fully carried out. But Bacon's capture of Jamestown changed everything. The councillor "drew up his Men in Battalia" before the statehouse and threatened to massacre all within unless they granted him authority to fight Indians. "God damne my Blood," he shouted, "I came for a comission, and a commission I will have before I goe." Berkeley and the assembly acceded to his demands. They named Bacon "generall and commander in cheife" of all provincial forces for the duration of the conflict and authorized him "to raise such number of volunteers for the more expeditious carrying on [of] this warr, as shall freely offer themselves for this service." He also was authorized to modify or cancel the assembly's latest war plan as he desired.[17]

Bacon proceeded cautiously at first. He decided to implement the assembly's plan but to use volunteers instead of pressed men whenever possible. Volunteers would, of course, be more enthusiastic, economical, and reliable (that is, loyal to Bacon) than draftees. But they were not always forthcoming. For example, the plan

16. A fort in Surry County was abandoned a short time earlier (June 5, 1676, *Statutes*, II, 341–53; June 5, 1676, *JHB*, II, 65; assembly to the king [June 5, 1676], CP, LXXVII, p. 324). One-eighth of the troops were to have been horsemen, a ratio developed in the conquest of the Irish "savages" a century earlier (Falls, *Elizabeth's Irish Wars*, 37).

17. Beverley, *History and Present State of Virginia*, 80; *Narratives*, 28–30, 116–17; June 5, 1676, *Statutes*, II, 349–50.

called for Northumberland County to provide forty-nine men for the northern force. Regimental officers selected the forty-nine from a list of names and ordered them "to be at Fairefeilds on Munday next And that the drums beate up for volunteers to goe out [on] the March against the Indians to be alsoe then in Fairefeilds And if their shall then Appeares volunteers to make up the Number of forty nine men, Then soe many of the men pressed as aforesaid, to be released, as there shall then and there appeares volunteers." Bacon may have had hundreds of followers in the southwestern counties, but he failed to arouse much interest on the Northern Neck. No volunteers appeared at Fairfields, and Northumberland County's dutiful but disgruntled selectees found themselves in service and on the public payroll for the next two months.[18]

The Northumberland muster and later events indicate that the northern column was composed largely of pressed men and the southern column mainly of volunteers. The original plan called for the two forces to operate independently, but Bacon was wary of such an arrangement. He decided to gather the entire force of a thousand men under his direct command at the falls of the James and from there march "into the Forest to Seek the Enemy." While preparations were going forward, word reached Bacon that an Indian war party had killed eight people along the Chickahominy River only twenty-three miles from Jamestown. The natives had penetrated so deeply partly because many Henrico, Charles City, and New Kent militiamen were in Jamestown with their rebel hero. Bacon immediately led his men out after the raiders, pausing only long enough to order militia officers in every county to raise "select companies of well armed men" from their depleted regiments and range the "Forists, swomps, thickits, and all such suspected places where the Indiands might have any shelter for the doeing of mischeife."[19] By early July perhaps fifteen hundred militiamen were in motion all across Virginia, patrolling the frontier, streaming toward the rendezvous site, or beating the bushes behind the lines.

18. July 4, 19, September 20, 1676, Northumberland County Records, Order Book, 1666–78, ff. 138, 141.

19. [Sherwood], "Virginias Deploured Condition," *Collections*, 172; Philip Ludwell to [?], June 28, 1676, CO 1/37, ff. 37–38; *Narratives*, 33–34, 55–56.

This outburst of activity raises the question of military expenses, which clearly was an issue in the rebellion. Yet not a single complaint has survived about the cost of the siege of the Susquehannock fort or the massive expedition devised by the June assembly and partially executed by Bacon. The uproar over money centered on Berkeley's abortive attempt in March to erect forts along the frontier. It seems that Virginians in 1676 were not so much opposed to military spending as to wasting a fortune on a porous, static system of defense which even the dullest Indian could penetrate. Bold counteroffensive moves that offered a chance for revenge and spoils apparently were acceptable no matter what the cost.

To this point the rebellion had been largely a test of will between Berkeley and Bacon over control and use of the provincial militia in the Susquehannock War. Now it slipped into a test of strength for control of Virginia. Shortly after Bacon marched away from Jamestown, the governor once more proclaimed the councillor a rebel and set about raising an army of his own. He crossed to the middle peninsula and summoned the remainder of the Gloucester and Middlesex regiments, the former generally considered "the best replenished for men, arms, and affections of any County in Verginia." When the militiamen had assembled before him, Berkeley announced his intention of leading them out to suppress the rebellion, by force of arms if necessary. But the settlers refused to fight "ther Country men neighboures and frinds" and simply walked away. Thus abandoned, Berkeley and his little band of loyalists fled to the Eastern Shore. At the falls, Bacon was impatiently awaiting the arrival of the northern forces when he heard of the events near the coast. Furious at what he deemed Berkeley's treachery, he wheeled about and marched east.[20]

Upon reaching Gloucester and learning that Berkeley was gone, Bacon moved quickly to consolidate his hold on the colony. He called a large number of planters together at Middle Plantation and urged them to take an oath to obey him and oppose the governor until the king could be informed of the situation. This bold move

20. *Narratives*, 34, 56–57, 119–21; Anne Cotton, "An Account of Our Late Troubles in Virginia," *Tracts*, I, 5; grievances of Isle of Wight County, March 8, 1676/7, CO 1/39, ff. 223–24.

created a furor, and a heated debate broke out. Then came word that a party of Indians was ravaging the middle peninsula and that Berkeley had carried off to the Eastern Shore all the ammunition stored in the redoubt on Gloucester Point. The planters at Middle Plantation were shocked that the governor should leave them without ammunition in the middle of a war against the common enemy and alarmed by the second deep Indian penetration of the summer. It was essential that the army take the field at once to drive the enemy away from the frontier and prevent further incursions. To speed Bacon on his way most of the planters signed the oath. Now Bacon truly held the "Militia of the country in his hands" for he seemed to be a general "by consent of the people" as well as by a commission from the government. He ordered local officers to step up their search for infiltrators and make "a generall Enrollment . . . through out the Country of all the house keepers and Freemen capable of bearing armes," an indication that Bacon was not yet considering a social revolution. He also sent "Parties of Horse Patrolling through every County, Carrying away Prisoners all whom he Distrusted," and dispatched a force across the bay to seize Berkeley.[21]

General Bacon then returned to "his favourite scheme of extirpating the Indians." He led his army back to the frontier, where a rendezvous was effected at last with the sluggish northern column. Then, instead of marching straight out against the Susquehannocks and other foreign Indians as he had promised to do, Bacon veered off toward a closer and more inviting target: the Pamunkeys.[22]

By midsummer the Pamunkeys had become alarmed at the deteriorating political situation in the colony and the increasingly violent rhetoric about "extirpating" Indians in general. Sometime in July they and several other subject tribes quietly abandoned their towns and withdrew into the swampy lowlands along the Piankatank River, undoubtedly hoping to ride out the approaching storm.

21. *Narratives*, 34, 58–64, 119–23; [Sherwood], "Virginias Deploured Condition," *Collections*, 172, 175–76; Cotton, "Account of Our Late Troubles," *Tracts*, I, 6–7; Nathaniel Bacon to John Washington, August 4, 1676, CP, LXXVII, p. 162.

22. *Virginia Gazette*, February 23, 1769; *Narratives*, 121–23.

The Pamunkey queen warned her people that "if they found the English coming upon them that they should neither fire a gun nor draw an arrow" but simply run away. Unfortunately, many colonists apparently saw the Pamunkeys' disappearance as proof of their complicity in the recent raids in New Kent and Gloucester. The result was a campaign against a people that in thirty years "had nere at any time betray'd or injuryed the English."[23]

Bacon's army marched from the falls to the "Freshes of York" and then northward to the upper Piankatank River, a dismal bog known as Dragon Swamp. The army, perhaps a thousand strong at this point, both horse and foot, volunteers and draftees, plunged into the swamp. The large column could not operate as a single unit in the dense woods, and Bacon "made them break the order of marching, and for expedition and conveniency to march at randome" in single file or in small packs. After a time the army's scouts (a dozen subject Indians of unknown lineage) came upon a cluster of huts. A group of dragoons attacked "in great disorder and hast" but not in time to prevent most of the Pamunkeys from escaping. The army pushed on and eventually found a second encampment with much the same result. Exhausted and exasperated, Bacon called a halt to take stock of the situation.[24]

The army had been in the field for two or three weeks and had killed or captured only ten Indians, seven of them women and children. Many of the troops, particularly the northern militiamen, were "tyred, Murmuring, impatient, half starved, dissatisfied," and altogether unhappy. Bacon decided to send them home before their "Murmuring" exploded into mutiny. He dismissed the entire northern column and with about four hundred southerners continued on, "hunting and beating the Swamps up and down" until supplies were practically exhausted and the expedition again ground to a halt. Bacon once more divided his forces, sent over half of his remaining men home, and pressed on with less than 150 volunteers. The very next day the English discovered and attacked the

23. *Narratives*, 123–25; Sir John Berry and Francis Moryson, "A List of the Names of those Worthy Persons, whose Services and Sufferings . . . have beene Reported to us most signal and Eminent," October 15, 1677, CO 5/1371, f. 181. Wertenbaker makes a fairly strong case against the Pamunkeys (*Torchbearer of the Revolution*, 145–46).

24. *Narratives*, 123–25; Leach, *Arms for Empire*, 58–59.

main Pamunkey camp. The natives "did not at all oppose, but fled, being followed by Bacon and his Forces killing and taking them Prisoners, and looking for the Plunder of the Field." Eight natives were killed and forty-five captured, mostly women and children. This wretched affair in Dragon Swamp was Bacon's second and final victory over friendly Indians. Burdened with plunder and prisoners, he led his exultant little band out of the swamp for what he doubtless expected would be a triumphal procession to Jamestown.[25]

Bacon must have been mightily astonished to learn that while he was in the swamp Governor Berkeley had returned from the Eastern Shore at the head of a sizable force and made himself master of Jamestown once again. The loyalists had used a ruse and "the juce of the Grape" to capture the ships and men Bacon had sent against them. This brief, bloodless action on the Eastern Shore was the turning point of the rebellion. It gave the loyalists control of the bay and the four great tidal rivers, and every heavily armed tobacco merchantman that entered the capes thereafter added the weight of its men and guns to the governor's cause. Berkeley wasted little time in taking advantage of this opportunity. He pressed most of the captive rebels into his own service and raised several hundred additional militiamen from Accomack and Northampton counties. He packed them aboard four ships and a dozen boats "and sailed with his whole fleet in triumph" to Jamestown. Bacon had posted eight hundred militiamen in the town, but when Berkeley called upon them to surrender they fell into "a ressalution of diserting the place" and did so almost immediately. The next day, September 8, the governor came ashore and proclaimed Bacon a rebel for the third time. Perhaps recalling the fiasco in Gloucester, Berkeley decided against leading a force out after Bacon. He ordered a palisade erected across the lower end of the neck of land connecting Jamestown to the mainland and settled down to await the arrival of his enemy.[26]

25. *Narratives*, 126–28; Sir John Berry and Francis Moryson, "A True Narrative of the Rise, Progresse, and Cessation of the late Rebellion in Virginia" [1677], CO 5/1371, f. 199; Cotton, "Account of Our Late Troubles," *Tracts*, I, 7.

26. *Narratives*, 64–67, 122, 128–29; *Virginia Gazette*, February 23, 1769; Wertenbaker, *Torchbearer of the Revolution*, 142, 186.

Bacon did not disappoint him. The rebels marched "in great fury" toward Jamestown, their ranks eventually swelling to about three hundred men, mostly from the southwest. After several forced marches this "Small tyr'd Body of men" arrived before the capital on the evening of September 13. Bacon halted his troops and boldly rode forward across the neck of land, really no more than a narrow sandbar, to reconnoiter the palisade on the other side. Seeing that a frontal assault by his little army would be suicidal, the general returned and ordered "a French worke to be cast up" where the neck of land joined the mainland. That night the rebels dug a trench and piled trees and brush in front of it to form a makeshift abatis. For the next two days the governor's vastly superior forces were content to harass them with occasional fire from the town and the ships. On the third day Berkeley made a disastrous error. Having failed to convince the rebels to surrender or dash themselves against his fortifications, he resolved to launch an assault of his own. On September 16 several hundred decidedly unenthusiastic loyalists set out toward the rebel earthworks. The barren neck afforded them neither cover nor room to maneuver. Bacon described how the governor's forces "made a salley with horse and foote, the foot in the Van[,] the forlorne [vanguard] being made up of such men as they had compelled to serve, they came on with a narrow front, and pressing very close, upon one anothers shoulders, that the forlorne might be theire shelter, our men received them soe warmely, that they retired in great disorder, throwing downe theire armes." The hail of "musquitt boolitts full in there faces" overwhelmed the conscripted militiamen who made up the bulk of the attacking force. Twelve loyalists were killed or wounded in the debacle "without one drop of Blood drawne from the enimy."[27]

This brief battle was the only engagement during the rebellion in which opposing forces engaged in something resembling a stand-up fight in the European tradition. The battle demonstrated the importance of tactics and morale in conflicts fought by amateurs.

27. *Narratives*, 68–70, 129–35; Nathaniel Bacon to William Cookson and Edward Sherm, September 17, 1676, CP, LXXVII, p. 216; *Virginia Gazette*, February 23, 1769; Cotton, "Account of Our Late Troubles," *Tracts*, I, 8; February 20, 1676/7, *JHB*, II, 69–70.

Militiamen in early Virginia, like militiamen in other times and places, usually fought best when they felt reasonably secure. Bacon's men had the same tactical and psychological advantages over their opponents as did later American militiamen at Bunker Hill and New Orleans. Berkeley's men, on the other hand, were called upon to perform that most difficult of all military maneuvers—a frontal assault upon a fortified position. Morale was an equally important factor. The rebels at Jamestown were certain they were in the right. The overwhelming majority of Berkeley's troops had no desire to kill or be killed by fellow Virginians whom they believed were trying to save the colony from the Indians. They were extremely reluctant soldiers, and their feelings were reflected in their assault on the rebel works. In the words of a contemporary wit, these militiamen "(like scholers goeing to schoole) went out with hevie harts, but returnd hom with light heeles."[28]

Soon after this "succeslesse Sally" the rebels obtained two cannons and began to pound away at the vulnerable palisade. To protect his little battery from counterfire and further demoralize his opponents, Bacon rounded up the wives and daughters of several of the gentlemen in Berkeley's party and placed them atop the parapet. He also displayed there the Pamunkeys captured on his recent foray into Dragon Swamp. This sight was too much for the governor's halfhearted followers. They slunk away to the ships leaving the old man practically alone in the town. Berkeley intended to die rather than desert his capital once again, but a handful of loyal gentlemen finally convinced him to retire with the rest to the Eastern Shore. The next day, October 19, the rebels entered Jamestown and burned it to the ground to prevent its recapture by the governor. Bacon and his men barely had begun to celebrate their victory when they learned that Colonel Giles Brent of Stafford County was leading a thousand men south to join Berkeley at Jamestown. The general quickly led his soldiers to Gloucester County to meet this new threat only to find that Brent's supporters had deserted him upon hearing of Berkeley's defeat and withdrawal.[29]

28. *Narratives*, 70.
29. *Ibid.*, 38, 71–73, 134–39; *Virginia Gazette*, February 23, 1769.

In routing the loyalists Bacon badly overplayed his hand. The burning of Jamestown was a great shock to the inhabitants of Virginia, but they received an even greater jolt when they learned that Bacon had begun enrolling white servants and black slaves into his army. A servant in Charles City County, John Finly, was "very often and earnestly urged and perswaded" by a "moste forward active rebell" named Wheeler to "beare armes for the rebell party, promissing him his freedome if he would soe doe." Finly refused, even after Wheeler imprisoned him for his obstinacy. But there were few servants and slaves with Finly's strength of character. Many more were like William Baker of York County, who "was a soldier in the late Rebellion with Bacon six weeks, being his owne voluntary Act." So many hundreds of servants and slaves joined the rebels that the population became alarmed. A loyalist had predicted earlier that if Bacon were so rash as to offer arms and freedom to bondsmen who joined him, "it will in a short time ruine him, since by it he will make all masters his Enimies." And that is what happened. Bacon's popular support withered away, and he was left with about a thousand men in arms, many without any military training or experience. The discredited, directionless rebellion soon degenerated into an orgy of looting and vandalism. The mixed lot of freemen, servants, and slaves "became *banditti* rather than soldiers" and ravaged the estates of their adversaries and many other colonists as well. Bacon began to exhibit "a more mercelesse severity and absolute authority" than before. Then Bacon died suddenly on October 26 in Gloucester County.[30]

Bacon's death was a mortal blow to the rebellion, which had no cause or focus other than his leadership and inflated reputation as an Indian fighter. One Joseph Ingram, an obscure newcomer to Virginia, appointed himself Bacon's successor and immediately made two critical errors. The first was to continue the fight. The second was to attempt to hold all that had been won. Ingram selected West

30. *Narratives*, 74, 94, 137–39; April 24, 1679, York County Records, No. 6, Deeds, Orders, Wills, Etc., 1677–84, p. 88; September 13, 1677, Charles City County Records, Orders, 1677–79, p. 190; February 20, 1676/7, *Statutes*, II, 395; Thomas Ludwell to the Privy Council [1676], CP, LXXVII, p. 332; Washburn, *Governor and the Rebel*, 209; *Virginia Gazette*, February 23, 1769; Boddie, *Colonial Surry*, 123–31.

Point as his main base and garrisoned it with several hundred men. He stationed another hundred at Green Spring, Berkeley's large plantation near Jamestown, and posted the remaining rebels along the lower York and James rivers. Ingram and his colleagues must have forgotten that the loyalists controlled the water. Scattering small groups along the tidal rivers was an open invitation to Berkeley to overwhelm them one at a time.[31]

For several weeks the loyalists had been staging minor hit-and-run raids on the western side of the bay. Learning of Bacon's death and the dispersal of the rebel forces, Berkeley increased the size and tempo of these waterborne attacks. In November he dispatched Robert Beverley, one of his most aggressive lieutenants, to Yorktown. Beverley landed there and "snapt up one Coll: Hansford and his party, who kep garde" on the bluffs. After delivering his prisoners to the Eastern Shore, he returned to Yorktown and captured a second band of rebels that had come to look for the first. Greatly encouraged by these and other successes, the governor assembled his growing fleet of merchantmen and once more set out across the bay.[32]

Five or six powerful merchant vessels entered the James River under the overall command of Robert Morris, captain of the *Young Prince*. These ships and their officers and seamen played a vital role in suppressing rebel forces on the south side. To cite but two examples, Captain Nicholas Prinne of the *Richard and Elizabeth* headed a landing party which "beat upp a Guard of the Rebells party at Cheepoke Creeke," and Captain John Consett of the *Mary* "with his owne hand shott that greate Rebell [William] Groves and with a few seamen disarmed and routed his whole party." As the ships moved up and down the river striking when and where they pleased, the rebels began to lose heart. In early December Morris and his seamen "went ashore and found some 200 men of the Enimies," who disbanded rather than fight. Another group of rebels which had fortified "Allens brick howse" (better known today as

31. *Narratives*, 78–86, 139; *Virginia Gazette*, February 23, 1769; Wertenbaker, *Torchbearer of the Revolution*, 184–86.

32. *Narratives*, 79–83; November 3, 1676, to January 1, 1676/7, *Statutes*, III, 567–69; Berry and Moryson, "List of Worthy Persons," f. 179.

Bacon's Castle) fled without offering any resistance. Heartened by these successes, loyalists and perceptive opportunists moved against the rebels. Skirmishes were fought in Nansemond, Isle of Wight, and Surry counties between settlers of opposing allegiances. As soon as he was able to distinguish friend from foe, Morris joined hands with the loyal forces. One day his seamen and "50 horse and 80 foot" from Surry County marched together against rebel troops, and on another occasion "the fleet" convoyed a party of Nansemond loyalists upriver to relieve an endangered outpost. By mid-January "the whole Southerne shore of James River was reduced to its former obedience" and the loyal forces there were awaiting news of Berkeley's campaign against the rebel center.[33]

The governor entered the York River aboard a flotilla of merchantmen intending to move toward the insurgent stronghold at West Point. He announced his return by unleashing Major Beverley, who surprised and captured his third rebel garrison, this one in Gloucester County. News of the raid sparked scattered, uncoordinated uprisings in Middlesex, Gloucester, and York counties, but the rebels were numerous and determined so near West Point, and they easily defeated the loyalists. The governor made no effort to aid his supporters and further injured his cause with a bungled attack on a rebel outpost in York County in which the loyalists were repulsed with numerous casualties. Stalled far short of his goal, Berkeley took another tack. He had learned that Thomas Grantham, captain of the merchant ship *Concord*, was slightly acquainted with Joseph Ingram. The canny old man therefore "resalved to try if he might not doe that by words, which others could not accomplish with Swords." He commissioned Grantham to meet with the rebel leaders and arrange a truce.[34]

Grantham's success as an intermediary was amazing. He soon convinced the nearest rebel commander, Gregory Walklett, to change sides and fight for the governor. Grantham suggested that Walklett ride to the anchorage at Gloucester Point "with a good Troope of

33. Sir John Berry and Francis Moryson, "Characters of the severall Commanders of Shipps," October 1, 1677, CO 1/41, f. 203; Robert Morris, "A Journal of the Time the Ship Young Prince was in the Kings Servis in James River" [1676–77], CO 1/37, ff. 180–89; *Virginia Gazette*, February 23, 1769; Boddie, *Seventeenth Century Isle of Wight County*, 148.

34. *Narratives*, 83–98.

Horse, and bring Armes for what Foot you can from West Point." The captain assured Walklett that the loyalist fleet at the point contained many "good fighting men to carry those Armes, and a consederable Company of resolved men to Assist you [al]ready Armed." Walklett did as advised, and the rebels lost one of their most effective troops of horsemen.[35]

Grantham next proceeded upriver to meet with Ingram and other rebel leaders. After a week of discussions Grantham recorded in his journal on January 2, 1677, that "Ingram and some of the Chiefe Officers made a Surrender of West Point to me, where was Foure great Gunns mounted, and about three hundred men with small Armes, and two Drums and two Colours. [I] Imediately dismounted the great Gunns, and perswaded the Souldiers to march to Generall Ingram's house, where I lodged a Barrell of Brandy for them to drinke, which they did, telling them I would come to them and give them the Oath of Obedience and assure them their pardon." The good captain then went two or three miles further up the Pamunkey River to the rebel magazine at Colonel John West's house. There he found "about foure hundred English and Negroes in Armes, who were much dissatisfied at the Surrender of the Point, saying I had betray'd them, and thereupon some were for shooting mee, and others for cutting me in peeces." After some very fast talking, the captain convinced most of the servants and slaves to surrender. They yielded up three cannons, five hundred muskets, hundreds of pounds of ammunition, and piles of plundered loot. Eighty slaves and twenty indentured servants refused to give in and attempted to make their way downriver to join a party of other diehards. Grantham was able to maneuver this obstinate group under the guns of a waiting merchantman and force them to lay down their arms. The capitulation of West Point and the magazine was soon followed by the surrender of Green Spring and the few remaining pockets of resistance. The rebellion was over.[36]

The Indian war went on a little longer. Unfortunately, almost

35. *Ibid.*, 92–96; [Thomas Grantham] to Gregory Walklett [January, 1677], CO 5/1371, f. 253; Berkeley to Gregory Walklett and proclamation by Berkeley, both January 1, 1676/7, CP, LXXVIII, p. 170; Thomas Grantham, "Accompt of my Transactions" [1677], *ibid.*, LXXVII, pp. 301–302.

36. Grantham, "Accompt of my Transactions," 301–302; *Narratives*, 92–98; Washburn, *Governor and the Rebel*, 86.

nothing is known of what happened on the frontier after September, 1676, because surviving accounts are concerned with the course of the rebellion. Bacon and Ingram were in effective control of most of the militia between July and December, but it does not appear that they made much effort to reinforce the frontier after the civil war began. Berkeley was preoccupied with other matters (primarily revenge) for the first few months of 1677, and he too left the frontier counties to shift for themselves. The assembly that met in February, 1677, observed only that the Indians "dayly continue to comitt" murders and other outrages. When Sir Herbert Jeffreys, acting as lieutenant governor for Thomas, Lord Culpeper, Berkeley's successor, finally took over in April, he invited nearby Indian leaders to Middle Plantation to make peace. The resulting treaty was similar to the one drawn up in 1646 except that the "severall scattered Remnants" of the Powhatan confederation were returned to their "ancient subjection" to the Pamunkeys, a reward to the queen of the Pamunkeys for her loyalty to the English despite Bacon's attack in Dragon Swamp. The treaty did not, however, halt all Indian depredations. No foreign Indians were invited to or attended the conference, and the frontier remained a dangerous place for some time to come.[37]

Governor Jeffreys brought with him more than a thousand infantrymen only to find the rebellion already over. These soldiers were the first British regulars dispatched to Virginia, but they were of no particular significance in the military history of the colony. The troops arrived unexpectedly at the worst possible time with "the whole Countrie soe Ruined and Desolate a place, and not a house left in James Towne to shelter them . . . and the Ground soe covered over with deepe snow and Ice, that it is almost impossible for men to subsist on shore." Because it was equally unhealthy for the soldiers to remain too long aboard their overcrowded transports, Jeffreys began returning them to England. Two groups were left be-

37. Sir John Berry and Francis Moryson, "A Particular Account" [October 15, 1677], CO 5/1371, f. 185; February 20, 1676/7, *Statutes*, II, 397; proclamation by Sir Herbert Jeffreys, April 27, 1677, CO 1/40, ff. 66–67; Sir John Berry and Francis Moryson to Mr. Watkins, May 4, 1677, CO 1/40, f. 130; "Articles of Peace," May 29, 1677, CO 1/40, ff. 202–203; Sir Herbert Jeffreys to Commissioners of Foreign Affairs, June 11, 1677, CP, LXXVIII, p. 64; Harrison, *Landmarks of Old Prince William*, 70–72.

hind. An unknown number of men were discharged and "sett free in the Country" at their own request. A hundred more—two companies of foot—were retained as a standing guard. These unfortunate soldiers seem to have been forgotten by authorities in London. No pay or provisions arrived after the first year, and the men of one company became mutinous. Finally, in mid-1682 the troops were paid off and discharged, bringing an end to the brief British military presence in seventeenth-century Virginia.[38]

The armaments Jeffreys and his regulars carried to the colony were of considerably greater importance. The June, 1676, assembly had asked the king for enough weaponry to equip an expeditionary force of a thousand infantry and six hundred horsemen. Similar urgent requests had been sent to London for forty years and always had been ignored. This time, however, the king was alarmed by the uproar in his oldest American dominion and ordered the Office of the Ordnance to send the colonists one thousand snaphance muskets and bandoliers, seven hundred carbines, five hundred "Hand-granados with fuzees," and a large amount of ammunition. A few months later the king authorized an additional five hundred muskets and bandoliers, one thousand swords and belts, fifteen hundred hand grenades, and an assortment of halberds, partizans, pikes, bills, drums, knapsacks, tents, bedrolls, axes, saws, and spades. Finally, a small "Traine of Artillery" was added, which included four brass three-pounders "Mounted on Travelling Carriages," two "Brass Morterpesces," and several hundred roundshot and mortar bombs. The artillery apparently was sent in response to the inability of the Virginians and Marylanders to reduce the Susquehannock fort. Much of this gear was used to fit out Jeffreys' regulars. When the soldiers returned to England or were discharged in Virginia their equipment was turned over to the colony.[39]

38. "The present State of the Soldiers designed for Virginia," November 1, 1676, CO 1/38, f. 58; Sir Herbert Jeffreys, Sir John Berry, and Francis Moryson to Sir Henry Coventry, February 14, 1676/7, CP, LXXVII, p. 104; Sir Herbert Jeffreys to [Sir Henry Coventry], February 11, 1677/8, April 2, 1678, *ibid.*, LXXVIII, pp. 206, 218; Philip Ludwell to [Sir Henry Coventry], July 19, 1679, *ibid.*, p. 407; Nicholas Spencer to the commissioners for trade and plantations, June 10, 1682, CO 1/48, ff. 317–18.

39. Sir Henry Coventry to Berkeley, July 14, 1676, British Library, Additional Manuscripts, 25120, f. 88; Office of the Ordnance, June 14, October 2, 24, November 7,

As they had done in 1622, British authorities specified that this material should be placed in a central armory for safekeeping. The Virginians were at first overwhelmed by the king's unexpected generosity and hastened to erect a pair of storehouses at Middle Plantation, the first "publique Magazine" in the colony since the 1620s. Once they recovered from their surprise and joy, however, the colonists realized the guns and ammunition would be of more use in the field than in a magazine fifty miles from the nearest frontier. They decided that the weaponry suitable for militia horse and foot should be "proportioned to every Respective County, according to theire nomber of Tythables," while the artillery, grenades, and other special gear remained in the magazine.[40]

The militia's performance in the third and last major Indian war of the century was unimpressive. Ineffective leadership, the amorphous nature of the conflict, and the colony's malignant internal problems combined to cripple Virginia's war effort. Local forces were aggressive—perhaps too aggressive—in the early stages of the conflict. Then the governor made a critical tactical and psychological error by stepping in and limiting the militia to a passive defensive role. A column or two of horsemen guided by subject Indians might have driven the Susquehannocks well away from the frontier or at least forced them onto the defensive. But Berkeley refused to authorize pursuit of the Susquehannocks. The people of Virginia clamored for permission to march, to lash out as they always had done in the past, and when permission was withheld they panicked and lashed out anyway, as much at the governor as at the Indians. In the end they did more damage to themselves and their allies than to the enemy.

The war and concurrent rebellion seriously disrupted the militia. Dozens of men were killed or wounded by Indians and hundreds

---

1676, CO 5/1355, pp. 68, 70–75; Sir Herbert Jeffreys to Berkeley, February 14, 1676/7, CO 5/1371, f. 48.

40. February 20, 1676/7, *JHB*, II, 71, 73. The mutinous company of regulars guarded the arms at Middle Plantation. When the company was disbanded in 1682 the equipment was moved, first to Colonel John Page's house, then to "the brick wind mill att Green Spring," and from there to a partially rebuilt Jamestown (June 21, 1682, March 13, 1682/3, *EJC*, I, 25, 45; Edward Randolph to William Blathwayt, March 14, 1692/3, WBP, II).

more were killed, wounded, imprisoned, mistreated, impoverished, or threatened by their fellows. Thousands deserted or changed sides—sometimes more than once—and respect for authority all but disappeared in some quarters. So much private military equipment was impressed or stolen and then lost that a number of units were effectively disarmed, a problem only partially alleviated by the distribution of the king's arms over the next few years. The internal organization of the militia disintegrated. Trainbands and associations disappeared, and well into the 1680s officials still were attempting to reform some of the county regiments into operational troops and companies.[41] Agricultural dislocations aggravated the already desperate economic situation and made it more difficult than ever to mount and sustain military operations. The political turmoil and bitter recriminations that followed left the military population demoralized and divided. Finally, and perhaps most distressing, the problem that triggered the rebellion—security from foreign Indians—was not resolved. The Virginia militia was never the same after 1676. It, too, was a victim of Bacon's Rebellion.

41. "A Copie of a Letter from Major Generall Smith to the 20 Colonels in Virginia touching the Militia," November 20, 1680, CO 1/46, ff. 112–13.

7. Decline

Less than a year after the peace conference at Middle Plantation a large number of Seneca Indians was sighted above the fall line. Seneca was the name Virginians gave to all members of the Five Tribes of the Iroquois, a powerful confederation whose homeland lay far to the north in western Pennsylvania and New York.[1] The colonists feared the Senecas or Iroquois and suspected with good reason that they had taken part in the recent Indian war, but this particular band professed friendship for the English and soon departed without incident. Relief was short-lived. In midsummer of 1678 a family of five on an isolated farm was nearly wiped out. Everyone naturally assumed the Senecas were responsible for this outrage, and "a very great terror" swept through the western counties.[2]

A few weeks later several dozen Senecas appeared at the head of the James River. Their intentions are unknown, but when the panic-stricken inhabitants of that area fled eastward the Indians helped themselves to food and other items. The disordered frontier militia forces responded vigorously but ineffectively. A small party of Charles City–Henrico dragoons arrived on the scene the next day and rode along the trail of plundered farms until it came to the uppermost house on the James. There the horsemen spied the Senecas and opened fire. The Indians made "a quick and sharp reply" which killed the two senior officers, Colonel John Epps and Major William Harris, and wounded two other troopers. Two Indians also were killed in the brief exchange of fire and another, a woman, was captured. Upon learning of this costly affair, Governor Jeffreys set out at once with "some of my owne Redcoats, and a considerable number of Horse" from the downriver counties to punish the "perfidious Heathen" but could find no trace of them. A second group

1. The Five Tribes were the Mohawk, Oneida, Onondaga, Cayuga, and Seneca. See Trelease, *Indian Affairs*, 12–24, 238–39; Colden, *History of the Five Indian Nations*, 20; Hunt, *Wars of the Iroquois*, 137–44.

2. Jeffreys to [Sir Henry Coventry], March 31, July 10, August 7, 1678, CP, LXXVIII, pp. 215, 273, 283.

of horsemen from the northern counties galloped off to pursue the natives but it, too, failed to bring them to battle. The Senecas made good their withdrawal northward, sniping at isolated farms as they went.[3] For the Virginians it was an inauspicious beginning to six years of skirmishing with the most powerful Indian confederation in English America.

The colony's options in dealing with the Senecas were limited. The militia was in no shape to fight another war, and even if it had been, traditional offensive operations—feedfights—clearly were impractical against an enemy whose towns and cornfields were two hundred miles distant. The only viable military alternative, and not a particularly attractive one in light of recent events, seemed to be to adopt a defensive stance and maintain a security force on the western frontier. In the spring of 1679 the authorities bypassed the shattered paramilitary system and ordered every forty tithables in the colony to "fitt and sett forth one able and suffitient man and horse . . . well and compleatly armed with a case of good pistolls, carbine or short gunn and a sword." Each group was to supply its horseman with ammunition and other provisions for an initial four months and to resupply him every four months thereafter. The 350 troopers so raised were to be stationed at four garrison houses or barracks on the Potomac, Rappahannock, Mattaponi, and James rivers and were to be paid a fixed monthly salary by their home counties. Four subject Indians were allotted to each outpost to act as guides and interpreters. This tactical approach was to be followed with only minor modifications for much of the next two decades.[4]

Nervous provincial authorities simultaneously adopted a conciliatory strategy. They dispatched two agents to New York to attempt to establish a truce with the Iroquois and, as a gesture of their goodwill, returned the Indian woman who had been captured. When another large Seneca war party was sighted above the falls

3. Jeffreys to [Sir Henry Coventry], [August, 1678], *ibid.*, pp. 293–94; Thomas Ludwell to [Sir Henry Coventry], June 16, 1679, *ibid.*, pp. 386–87; September 21, 1678, *Minutes*, 78; October 22, 1679, Northumberland County Records, Order Book, 1678–98, p. 48; Colden, *History of the Five Indian Nations*, 21–26.

4. April 25, 1679, *Statutes*, II, 433–40; June 7, 1679, Northumberland County Records, Order Book, 1678–98, pp. 37–38.

of the James in July, 1679, authorities hastily sent a delegation upriver to assure the Indians of Virginia's friendly intentions. These gestures, officials hoped, would make the Senecas "more shye of Attacking us."[5]

The success of these peaceful overtures would not be known for some time, so the Virginians selected and outfitted the frontier garrisons and sent them on their way. Within a few months problems developed. When the time came for the first resupply, the "forties" supporting the militiamen were "very much dificient in their provisions and other necessaryes," and the counties proved to be no better in paying salaries. Discipline quickly collapsed. Many soldiers rode home when their food ran out or their pay failed to arrive. Some who were paid also left, such as Benjamin Clifton of the Mattaponi garrison, who "privately absented himself" when he became disenchanted with frontier life.[6]

The winter of 1679–1680 was unexpectedly quiet. The only serious trouble came in January, when another family on the upper James was massacred. The troopers stationed at the falls failed to detect or prevent the incursion but afterward dutifully "went in search of the Assassinators." Native guides led the colonists westward to a village of "Remote Indians" of unknown identity. Seven Indian men allegedly confessed to the murders and were executed on the spot. This affair seemed all too similar to the incident that had precipitated the Susquehannock conflict, and officials in Jamestown worried that they might have another "National Warr" on their hands, but no repercussions were recorded.[7]

When word arrived in the spring of 1680 that a peace treaty had been negotiated in Albany with the Five Tribes, most Virginians reacted cautiously at first. One guardedly observed that "we are at present very quiet from our Indian Enemies," and another would

5. Chicheley to [Lord Culpeper], July 13, 1679, CP, LXXVIII, p. 396; Philip Ludwell to [Sir Henry Coventry], June 16, July 19, 1679, *ibid.*, pp. 386–87, 406; Colden, *History of the Five Indian Nations*, 28–31. Virginia was party to an unsuccessful treaty made with the Iroquois by the Maryland government in 1677 (Trelease, *Indian Affairs*, 239–41).

6. January 27, February 24, 1679/80, York County Records, No. 6, Deeds, Orders, Wills, Etc., 1677–84, pp. 180, 198.

7. Nicholas Spencer to [Sir Henry Coventry], January 15, 1679/80, CP, LXXVIII, p. 438, and to [?], March 18, 1679/80, CO 1/44, f. 131.

only say that the colony had made "as firm a peace with the Northern Indians as with Indians can bee concluded." Nevertheless, the treaty seemed reason enough to reduce the burden of the garrisons. The price of tobacco was plunging so low one Virginian reported, "There is very little difference betweene the planters working and sitting still." A major cutback in military spending was inevitable.[8]

The assembly met in June and reduced the size of the four frontier garrisons to twenty men apiece. The troopers were still to be paid out of county funds, but their provisions henceforth would be supplied by large planters such as William Byrd, who would in turn be reimbursed by the provincial government. Sir Henry Chicheley, lieutenant governor in the absence of Lord Culpeper, was authorized to replace up to half of the militiamen in each garrison from the two companies of British regulars. Because the regulars were paid by the crown when they were paid at all, this exchange would further reduce the burden on Virginia's taxpayers. Chicheley soon decided to exercise this option. By the end of 1680 the Old Dominion's feeble front-line defense consisted of forty-eight "Country Soldiers," thirty-two "Redcoats," and a few Indians.[9]

In 1682 the older portions of the colony were thrown into turmoil by a rebellion that began in Gloucester County. Many farmers hoped to raise the disastrously low price of tobacco by limiting production. When the assembly failed to legislate a reduction in the size of the current crop, some of them took matters into their own hands. Between May and August the middle peninsula was caught up in an orgy of destruction as thousands of young tobacco plants were cut down. Outraged planters whose crops had been ravaged then hastened to do the same to their neighbors so that none would have an advantage.[10]

Chicheley faced a ticklish situation. He was aware of the widespread dissatisfaction with economic conditions and, as a former prisoner of Bacon's rebels, he knew firsthand the government's vulnerability to insurrection. He ordered some of the king's arms that

8. William Fitzhugh to Francis Partis, June 11, 1680, in Davis, ed., *William Fitzhugh*, 80; Nicholas Spencer to Sir Henry Coventry, July 9, 1680, CO 1/45, f. 189.

9. June 8, 1680, *Statutes*, II, 469–71; July 8, 22, August 3, 1680, *EJC*, I, 6, 10–12.

10. Morgan, *American Slavery*, 284–88.

had been distributed to needy counties five years earlier returned to the relative security of Middle Plantation. He then ordered Colonel Matthew Kemp of the partially reorganized Gloucester regiment to suppress the rioters with his militiamen but cautioned him to mobilize only "soe many of them as may, in this juncture, bee admitted to arms." Similar orders were sent to regimental commanders in adjoining counties as the cutting spread. Virginia's rulers were wary of mobilizing the ragged rank and file of the militia because they believed Bacon's Rebellion had infected the lower reaches of the population with an "Itching desier" to revolt. Consequently, it seems that Kemp and other officers called upon only the more prosperous and presumably more reliable mounted forces to restore order. The "militia horse" eventually did just that, and the plant cutting subsided. This outburst of lawlessness was the last serious internal upheaval in Virginia until the end of the colonial period.[11]

The disbanding of the regulars in the midst of the plant-cutting uproar was an unexpected complication because it meant that the cost of maintaining the four frontier garrisons at full strength would increase in the future. Because this news would hardly have a calming effect on the populace, Virginia's leaders decided to abolish the garrisons altogether. The next assembly again bypassed the regular militia structure and created four ranger companies, which bore a marked resemblance to the now-defunct trainbands of the 1650s and 1660s. Stafford, Rappahannock, New Kent, and Henrico counties were to raise a company of twenty men each, "well furnished with horses and all other accoutrements" with a responsible "housekeeper" to "command, lead, traine, conduct and exercise" each company. The men of each unit were to muster and drill once a month and to "range and scout about the frontiers" of their home county at least once every two weeks. Should suspicious foreign natives be encountered the company was to follow them but

11. "An Account of Ordnance Armes and Stores of War at Virginia," May 23, 1681, March 3, 1682/3, EP, III; Chicheley to the king, May 8, 1682, CO 5/1356, p. 66; May 3, 1682, *EJC*, I, 18–19; Chicheley to Sir Lionel Jenkins, May 31, 1682, CO 1/48, f. 275; Nicholas Spencer to Sir Lionel Jenkins, May 30, June 7, August 12, 1682, CO 1/48, ff. 261, 313, CO 1/49, f. 106; Breen, "Changing Labor Force," 3–25; Rainbolt, "Alteration in the Relationship," 410–34.

not to engage them unless they "shall obstinately persist to commit acts of hostility." The rangers would live at home and would not have to be housed, fed, and clothed at public expense, though they would be paid a salary by the provincial government. As resident frontiersmen they would be familiar with the terrain and the local natives and might be expected to take a keen interest in the security of their stretch of the border. Robert Beverley summed up the reasoning behind the creation of this force when he wrote that these "small Parties of Light Horse. . . . might afford to serve at easier Rates, and yet do the Business more effectually" than the garrisons. During the fall of 1683 the colony was visited by a group or groups of Senecas, who "riffled some houses" and attacked the Mattaponi and Chickahominy tribes in spite of the treaty. Details are scarce, but it is known that the new ranger-trainbands engaged in "constant rangings" and pursuits as long as the weather permitted.[12]

The arrival of Francis Howard, Baron of Effingham, the new governor, in 1684 marked the beginning of the final stage in the history of the seventeenth-century Virginia militia. Effingham was unimpressed by the informal ranger-trainbands and positively distressed by the "unsettled condition" of the rest of the provincial forces. He urged his first assembly to "Methodize" the militia so that it might become "serviceable in secureing the Country" once again. It is not clear what suggestions the governor made to the legislators because they responded with an apparently unrelated smattering of military legislation. The assembly ordered that regimental musters henceforth be held on a regular basis, though there is no evidence that this was ever done. The assembly next replaced the ranger-trainbands with a slightly larger and more expensive "standing force" of 120 troopers divided into the usual four companies. Requirements and salaries were much the same as before with two exceptions: the men were to be quartered in their own or other private homes "as near together as possible" and were to patrol the frontier once a week. The assembly also prohibited the

12. November 10, 1682, *Statutes*, II, 498–501; Beverley, *History and Present State of Virginia*, 95; September 17, November 21, 29, 1683, October 25, 1684, *EJC*, I, 52, 54, 67; May 5, 10, 1684, *JHB*, II, 209, 218.

impressment of private military equipment. This technique of ensuring that men on the march were fully armed had been badly abused during Bacon's Rebellion, when a large amount of personal equipment was pressed or confiscated, often illegally and often by desperate characters, and never returned. The new law was designed to encourage Virginians to purchase their own arms. The assembly then provided further encouragement by ordering all freemen without arms to correct that deficiency by 1686 or be fined, an order that was ignored by many in the impoverished population. This session of the assembly is particularly noteworthy because the legislators referred to the thousands of regular militiamen as "auxillaries" to the small, semimercenary frontier forces instead of the other way around.[13] Times and attitudes were changing.

The summer of 1684 was quiet, and Effingham sailed to New York to escape Virginia's heat and to meet with the Iroquois sachems at Albany. The Indian leaders acknowledged the recent raids on Virginia but declared truthfully that they had little control over wide-ranging parties of young warriors, who were like "wolfs in the woods" in search of prey. They promised, however, to make an effort to curb such activities in the future. After a considerable amount of speechmaking the hatchet was reburied. William Byrd and four tidewater chiefs journeyed to Albany the following year to remind the Iroquois that the treaty included the subject tribes, who by now were so "wasted and dwinled away" they relied almost completely on the Virginians for protection.[14] The time, trouble, and money expended on these voyages were well spent, for the Five Tribes generally refrained from violating the terms of the peace

13. Effingham to the House of Burgesses, April 19, 1684, EP, II; April 16,1684, *Statutes*, III, 13–14, 17–22. Two examples of "poore mens Armes prest from them . . . and so lost" are in grievances of Gloucester County [February, 1676/7], CO 1/39, f. 244, and Isle of Wight County, March 8, 1676/7, CO 1/39, f. 224.

14. Effingham to the Earl of Sunderland [August, 1684], CO 5/1356, pp. 298–99; "Proposition or Oration of the Onnondages and Cayouges Sachims," August 2, 1684, CO 1/66, f. 326; treaty between Virginia and the Five Tribes, July 30, 1684, and Effingham to the House of Burgesses, November 9, 1685, EP, I; Trelease, *Indian Affairs*, 259–60; May 1, 1688, *EJC*, I, 94–95. Trelease points out that "neither outside pressure nor the policy of the [Iroquois] sachems could prevent war parties from setting out wherever and whenever it pleased them" (*Indian Affairs*, 258).

after 1685; occasional sniping continued, but serious Anglo-Indian conflict in seventeenth-century Virginia was over.[15]

The outbreak of peace encouraged Effingham to press ahead with his plans to remodel the militia, though it appears that those plans had changed somewhat since his first meeting with the assembly. The governor now seemed at least as interested in enhancing the militia's political reliability as he was in reviving its military capability. The legislators proved to be an obstacle. Arguing that military expenses and innovations should be minimal in peacetime, they pressured the governor into disbanding the four companies on the frontier and then refused for more than five years to provide a replacement force. A second stalemate developed over the militia. In early 1687 Effingham and the council complained to London that the assembly repeatedly blocked efforts "to forme the Militia, as In tyme of danger to render it usefull for the defence of the country against our wild Indian Enimies, or other forreigne Enimies and alsoe to make it as u[s]efull to unruly home spirits." This last phrase referred not only to the uprisings in 1676 and 1682 but also to the recent restlessness in the colony caused by news of Monmouth's abortive rebellion in England; it is the key to understanding Effingham's motives. He did not intend to be the third royal governor driven out of Virginia in fifty years; he was attempting to fashion a means of preserving law and order from the paramilitary materials at hand.[16]

Rebuffed by the assembly, Effingham began to tinker with the militia on his own authority as supreme military commander in the colony. He was determined to bring the Virginia forces into line "as neer as the Constitution of this Government will beare to the Kingdom of England," where the later Stuarts were using the de-

15. Several instances of small-scale sniping after 1685 are related in Davis, ed., *William Fitzhugh*, 232, and Tinling, ed., *Correspondence*, I, 107–108, 111–12, 120–22, 145.

16. Rainbolt, "New Look at Stuart 'Tyranny,'" 387–406; November 26, 27, 1685, journal of the House of Burgesses, EP, I; October 20, 1686, *Statutes*, III, 38; November 12, 1686, *JHB*, II, 281; Effingham to the king, February 22, 1686/7, CO 5/1357, pp. 125–26; Nicholas Spencer to the lords commissioners for trade and plantations, February 2, 1686/7, CO 1/61, f. 206.

caying national militia primarily to suppress domestic turmoil. He ordered a list made of "all the ablest Freeholders and Inhabitants in their respective Counties that are Quallified either in Estate or person . . . to be listed in a Troope for that County . . . and likewise an account of all other Freeholders and Inhabitants that are fitt to be Listed for Foot." By "fitt" Effingham meant ownership of the equipment necessary to be a dragoon or infantryman. Those thousands of freemen who had been unable or unwilling to comply with the 1684 ordinance concerning weapons soon found themselves relegated to an unarmed general reserve much like that in England. The cut in military manpower was so dramatic the old regimental system—apparently largely defunct since Bacon's Rebellion—finally was discarded. Most counties now fielded only a single troop of horse and a single company of foot; some could not do that well. In 1680 the disorganized postrebellion militia contained more than eighty-five hundred men; nine years later it had been pared down to about forty-three hundred. In 1680 "scarce one half" of the militiamen were armed; nine years later the troops in the reduced force were "for the most part Compleatly Equipt." Lord Howard no doubt congratulated himself on solving the weapons shortage and easing the problem of political instability by the simple expedient of limiting the militia to relatively prosperous men with arms. The exclusionary trend that had begun decades earlier now had reached its zenith: an English-style "bourgeois militia" was emerging on American soil.[17]

The militia now began to acquire trappings hitherto rare in the Old Dominion. At the governor's express order the county commanders in chief, as the former regimental commanders now were styled, set about obtaining "Military ornaments" for their small, select units. The results must have been impressive and not a little startling. Even so isolated an area as Rappahannock County pur-

17. Millar, "Militia and the Army," 69–79; October 3, 1686, *LJC*, I, 111–12; October 24, 1687, *ibid.*, 85–86; "A Copie of a Letter from Major Generall Smith to the 20 Colonels in Virginia touching the Militia," November 20, 1680, CO 1/46, f. 112; Effingham to the lords commissioners for trade and plantations, May 28, 1689, CO 5/1358, p. 1.

chased gilded halberds, silk pennants and flags, brass trumpets, and gaily bedecked drums for its backwoods forces. At least one wealthy planter was pleased with the changes, believing that "a full number with a Soldier like appearance, is far more suitable and commendable, than a far greater number presenting themselves in a field with Clubs and staves, rather like a Rabble Rout than a well disciplined Militia." As is practically always the case in early Virginia it is not recorded how the "rabble" felt, but undoubtedly a good many, like their English cousins, were glad to be rid of an occasionally burdensome responsibility.[18]

By 1689 the militia was better organized than at any time since Berkeley's day, but it was far smaller and as much or more a constabulary as a combat force. It resembled its English counterpart in form and function more closely than ever before. Just how effective it might have been in a civil or military crisis will never be known because it was not tested, though Effingham seems to have been pleased with it. The governor declared that when he came to Virginia he found the militia "in great Disorder, or indeed in no order at all . . . Yet now I hope it is [as] good as ever, that I shall be prepared against any Insurrection or Invasion."[19] His successors would not be so optimistic.

In 1689 Effingham was recalled, and the able soldier and administrator Sir Francis Nicholson was dispatched to Virginia as lieutenant governor. Nicholson's appointment coincided with the outbreak of King William's War, the beginning of the long Anglo-French struggle for dominance in North America. When he arrived in Virginia in mid-1690 the lieutenant governor found the colonists shaken by reports of French and Indian depredations in New York and New England. Nicholson quickly set out to inspect the frontier defenses and discovered to his dismay that "the Militia was not in Such Condition as it ought." The veteran officer was especially disturbed at the large number of unarmed, untrained freemen who

18. William Fitzhugh to Nicholas Spencer, February 16, 1687/8, in Davis, ed., *William Fitzhugh*, 238; February 2, 1687/8, Rappahannock County Records, Order Book, 1686–92, p. 62; Bruce, *Institutional History*, II, 44.

19. Effingham to Lord Sunderland, May 22, 1688, EP, II.

were not enrolled in the militia. He resurrected the 1684 statute concerning weapons but soon learned that such directives had little effect in impoverished Virginia. Nicholson next appealed vainly to the English government for a massive influx of arms and ammunition so that even the "poore and Indigent" inhabitants of the Old Dominion could participate in its defense. Members of the colony's ruling elite were somewhat disconcerted at the lieutenant governor's abortive attempt to arm the poorer sort and incorporate them once again into the militia, but they were sufficiently concerned about the threat of an Indian attack to agree to the expense of reestablishing four small companies of mounted troops at the heads of the rivers. These little bands patrolled the frontier from 1691 to 1698, by which time the war had ended.[20]

No other colonial governor, except possibly Berkeley in his younger days, gave the militia such close attention as did Nicholson. He repeatedly made exhausting trips around the perimeter of the colony and even into neighboring Maryland "mustering, exercising, and personally inspecting" men and equipment. One impressed planter observed that whenever a portion of the colony was afflicted by "Rumours of danger, commotion or accidents" the lieutenant governor was "soon on the place in person" to set things right. But after a time Nicholson acknowledged that his whirlwind visits were intended mainly to bolster the "Drooping Spirits" of the settlers, for he came to realize that without substantial assistance from England he could do little to improve the colony's security. Fortunately, there were no major enemy incursions during Nicholson's brief tour of duty in Virginia, only the occasional incidents of thievery and violence which were an accepted part of life on the early frontier.[21]

20. Nicholson to lords commissioners for trade and plantations, August 20, [October] 1690, CO 5/1358, pp. 20, 42–43; May 1, June 4, July 24, October 23, 1690, January 15, 1690/91, *EJC*, I, 111–14, 117–18, 120–21, 132–34, 141–42; William Byrd to Effingham, June 10, 1689, and to Arthur North, July 23, 1689, in Tinling, ed., *Correspondence*, I, 107–108, 111–12; William Cole to William Blathwayt, August 1, 1690, January 28, 1690/91, WBP; April 16, 1691, September 24, 1696, *Statutes*, III, 82–84, 164.

21. J.M. to William Blathwayt, June 30, 1692, WBP; Nicholson to William Blathwayt, June 10, 1691, *ibid.*; Nicholson to lords commissioners for trade and plantations, November 4, 1690, January 26, 1690/91, February 26, 1691/2, July 16, 1692, CO

The status quo continued during the first years of the governorship of Sir Edmund Andros, which began in the fall of 1692. Like Nicholson, Andros was an experienced soldier and administrator who was distressed at the condition of Virginia's defenses. He toured the backcountry shortly after his arrival and found the militia generally unimpressive and the inhabitants "very Indifferently Armed." Perhaps discouraged by how little the energetic Nicholson had been able to accomplish, or perhaps more concerned with the French than the Indians, Andros soon turned his attention to the rehabilitation of Virginia's decrepit coastal fortifications and the construction of a magazine at Jamestown.[22]

Serious violence flared again during the summer of 1694, when unidentified Indians killed a settler near the falls of the James. Following several relatively quiet years, this incident threw the western counties into turmoil. The government at Jamestown responded by raising thirty-six additional men for frontier duty and urging militia officers in exposed areas to be vigilant and bold. Despite these precautions another settler was killed by "strange sculking Indians" the following year. In both instances the attackers—probably small bands of Senecas—approached and escaped undetected. Andros attempted to rally the colonists by example and exhortation and then took the dramatic step of reincorporating the poorer freemen into the active militia. He apparently concluded that in time of war it was vital to expose these people to at least rudimentary military training, regardless of whether they had the proper equipment and how they were viewed by the more established planters. Exactly how this reorganization was carried out is not known, though it appears most of the newcomers were formed into separate troops and companies which the governor aptly described as being "unsuiteably (and not well) Armed." By 1696 or 1697 the enlarged provincial militia consisted of eighty-three hundred men organized into forty troops of horse and eighty-three

---

5/1358, pp. 29, 37, 153, 207; William Byrd to Daniel Horsmanden, July 25, 1690, and to Effingham, January 23, 1691/2, in Tinling, ed., *Correspondence*, I, 121–22, 145.

22. Andros to lords commissioners for trade and plantations, November 3, 1692, July 22, 1693, CO 5/1358, pp. 224, 242–43; Andros to William Blathwayt, November 3, 1692, January 16, 1692/3, WBP.

companies of foot.[23] In numbers, if nothing else, the militia was a formidable force once more.

Unfortunately, what may seem to have been a landmark in the evolution of the militia was, in fact, an episode of no particular significance. The active militia—Effingham's "bourgeois militia"—continued as before to be the core of the colony's paramilitary institution, especially after the frontier forces were disbanded at the close of King William's War. The reserve militia—the poorer freemen—continued as before to be an embarrassment and, for some, a cause for concern. In short, little had changed except for the reappearance of a severe weapons shortage within the militia. Nevertheless, Andros probably would have agreed with the planter who concluded that the governor had "putt the Militia into the best posture it will admitt" under the circumstances.[24] He could not work miracles. The militia was a prisoner of its past.

The treaty with the Iroquois, the gradually improving domestic political situation, and the lull in the conflict with France allowed many Virginians to convince themselves that a reliable militia was an expensive luxury they could do without. Succeeding executives made repeated efforts to reinvigorate and even expand the militia but accomplished little in the face of such complacency. Lieutenant Governor Alexander Spotswood summed up the situation in 1712 when he declared that by some "unaccountable infatuation, no arguments I have used can prevail upon these people to make their Militia more Serviceable, or to fall into any other measures for the Defence of their Country." The militia naturally began to atrophy in this indifferent environment: musters were held less frequently and were less well attended, military titles and offices grew increasingly honorific, and distinctions between active and reserve forces gradually blurred. By the second decade of the eigh-

23. Andros to William Blathwayt, July 20, September 12, 1694, August 10, 1695, WBP; August 23, 1694, Henrico County Records, Deeds and Wills, 1688–97, p. 432; Andros to Council of Trade and Plantations, July 1, 1697, CO 5/1359, p. 121; August 12, 1696, York County Records, No. 10, Deeds, Orders, Wills, Etc., 1694–97, p. 328; "Answers of Sir Edmund Andros to the Queries of the Council of Trade and Plantations," August 20, 1697, CO 5/1359, pp. 41, 118.

24. Ralph Wormeley to William Blathwayt, August 18, 1695, WBP.

teenth century the "weak and defenceless condition" of the colony was well known, and the militia was considered to be "the worst in the King's Dominions."[25] The days when royal governors of Virginia could call forth a host of "Fyghtinge men" were over.

25. Morgan, *American Slavery*, 352–55; Spotswood, *Official Letters*, II, 1–8, 34, 41–42, 212; Robert Quary and Dionysius Wright, "The state and Condition of . . . Virginia as to fortifications and state of defence," January, 1701/2, CO 5/1312, f. 158; Hartwell, Blair, and Chilton, *Present State of Virginia*, 63–64; Beverley, *History and Present State of Virginia*, 253, 268–70; Shy, "New Look at Colonial Militia," 175–85.

Conclusion

The transfer of the English paramilitary system to the New World was not inevitable. A protomilitia was formed in the first years of the Virginia colony because the Virginia Company could not afford a more professional, that is, more expensive means of security for its overseas outpost. Had an adequate mercenary force or royal garrison been established at Jamestown, our story might have turned out differently. As it was, after several false starts a recognizable if rudimentary militia finally emerged after the first massacre in response to the dangerous conditions that characterized frontier life.

In certain ways the early militia closely resembled the great fyrd of bygone days, which is not entirely surprising because seventeenth-century Virginians faced conditions similar in many respect to those experienced by their Anglo-Saxon ancestors. Both peoples lived in isolated and relatively simple societies which were threatened frequently by powerful, elusive enemies, and both societies depended to some degree for their survival on militias composed of adult males who were expected to take up arms in times of danger. Thus, although Virginia's embryonic paramilitary force fairly bristled with contemporary English terminology and weaponry, its fyrdlike militancy and composition distinguished it sharply from its counterpart across the Atlantic. The early Virginia militia might best be described as an anachronistic institution based on the hoary concept of the nation in arms, a not so faint echo of an embattled England a millennium in the past. It was both the sword and shield of the Old Dominion: an expeditionary force, main line of defense, and reserve of last resort all in one. And, in the final analysis, it made the difference, not merely between victory and defeat but between survival and annihilation.

Such was not the case, of course, in Stuart England. At the advent of colonization the national militia was by practically any standard a decadent, obsolescent institution. Only a small fraction of the able-bodied males in the realm participated, with varying degrees of skill and enthusiasm, in occasional musters. The remainder of the military population was relegated to the status of an inactive reserve. During the latter half of the seventeenth century the national militia served as little more than a rough and ready constabulary force that helped maintain internal order by suppressing riots and rebellions, particularly in the countryside. Its limited mission decidedly did not include posing as a bulwark against invasion except, perhaps, in the last extremity. The kingdom's external security rested on its insularity, alliances, and "wooden walls."

The Virginia militia passed through several stages during its initial hundred years of existence. The first quarter of the seventeenth century was a period of uncertainty and experimentation, which eventually produced a workable paramilitary system. During the second quarter of the century this system was reorganized, refined, and repeatedly tested in combat. In the third quarter of the century the militia attained its most sophisticated form with the appearance of regiments, special units, and regional associations but was greatly reduced in size by the exclusion of most servants and slaves. This elaborate structure came crashing down during Bacon's Rebellion and was replaced in the final quarter of the century by a smaller and more exclusive system. Even this emasculated version of the militia steadily deteriorated as Virginians came to rely for their security on diplomacy and the regular forces of the empire. And so the militia languished through much of the eighteenth century until revived by the fires of revolution.

Undoubtedly the most striking feature of the militia was its rapid, continuous evolution. Virginians did not hesitate to adjust familiar English martial practices to fit the unfamiliar requirements of the New World, nor did they hesitate to alter their paramilitary system as times and circumstances changed. Indeed, developments in early Virginia roughly paralleled and in some instances nearly duplicated the English paramilitary experience from Alfred the Great to William and Mary but did so in a fraction of the time.

Another of the militia's notable characteristics was its predominantly offensive, or counteroffensive, orientation. From the early raids of Smith and Dale to those of Berkeley and Bacon decades later, the colonists defended themselves by pounding away at their enemies. The march and the feedfight—two marvelously expressive words far removed from today's antiseptic military jargon—were the twin hallmarks of military operations for much of the century. Virginia's aggressive strategy and harsh tactics were developed and perfected in the colony's first years as part of a calculated policy of intimidation against the Indians. This approach was continued in later years partly out of habit and partly out of necessity because of the colonists' vulnerable manner of dispersed settlement. The march and the ensuing feedfight made the natives look to their own homes and crops and provided colonial soldiers with an opportunity for revenge and spoils (no small matter in a poor country). In Virginia the best defense was a good offense. Whenever colonial counterstrokes failed to materialize, as in the spring of 1676, real and psychological pressure on the exposed frontier residents became unbearable. For seventy years Virginians strove to destroy their enemies or drive them away. The shift to a defensive posture after Bacon's Rebellion came about largely because the colonists had conquered or cowed all the native peoples within reasonable striking range.

Closely related to the militia's offensive orientation was its inclusive nature. For decades practically every adult male in Virginia was required by law to attend musters and stand ready to defend the province. A certain effort on our part is needed to understand how unusual the militia's inclusiveness was in the context of the times. In seventeenth-century Europe a mass militia was considered an anachronism, and a dangerous one at that. Organizing peasants into martial bands and training them in the use of modern weapons seemingly flew in the face of common sense by inviting insurrection. Nevertheless, that is exactly what was done in early Virginia and, so great was the fear of the Indians, it was done without any signs of distress on the part of provincial authorities. As Virginia expanded after mid-century an enormous surplus of military manpower developed, and a mass militia no longer seemed essential. About the same time Virginia's well-to-do planters belatedly began to fear a possible uprising of the restless, impoverished, and partially armed underclasses. The result was the gradual exclusion from the militia of various segments of the population: most slaves in the 1640s, most servants in the 1650s, and, for all practical purposes, most poorer freemen in the 1680s. In its twilight at the close of the seventeenth century the provincial paramilitary system—or at least its core, the active militia—was nearly as exclusive as the one in England.

The dispersed pattern of settlement, the chronic danger of Indian incursions, and the inclusive composition of the militia led to an extraordinarily widespread distribution of firearms in the colony up to about mid-century or slightly later. The only practical way to equip militiamen living on scattered farmsteads in hostile country was to ensure that each had his own complement of weapons close at hand. This decision was a sharp break with English practices. After Bacon's Rebellion there were second thoughts, and some authorities in London and Jamestown attempted to reestablish central magazines and thereby limit the distribution of firearms, but these efforts were not particularly successful. The relative decline in the number and distribution of firearms after mid-century was primarily the result of changing social and economic patterns.

Virginians often employed weapons differently than did their English cousins. Clumsy polearms quickly were abandoned in favor of the latest firearms, especially the relatively lightweight snaphance models. Swords and sabers similarly gave way, though more slowly, to multipurpose edged weapons such as axes and hatchets. On the other hand, metal body armor remained in general use somewhat longer than in Europe. Information on tactics is more difficult to come by, but it appears that militia forces in Virginia adopted loose, irregular formations for use against Indians and perhaps against Europeans as well. Dutch landing parties in 1667 probably were repulsed by militiamen deployed in the woods in such a fashion. More traditional European formations were retained and practiced assiduously but were used only on muster days and other ceremonial occasions. The one major known exception was Berkeley's ill-advised frontal assault against entrenched rebels at Jamestown in 1676.

The Old Dominion's numerous internal problems adversely affected its ability to maintain a viable paramilitary institution in the second half of the seventeenth century. The most serious difficulty was the colony's chronically depressed economy. It is no exaggeration to say that the militia's most formidable foe was poverty, not Indians or Europeans. Poverty crippled the militia in a variety of direct and indirect ways. It was the principal reason why a growing number of people could not arm themselves, why the colony could not erect and maintain suitable coastal fortifications, and why servants and poorer freemen became so disgruntled over their present condition and future prospects that they were considered by many other Virginians to be more of a threat than were the natives. The militia also was undone to a considerable degree by its own success. The establishment of absolute military supremacy in the tidewater region and the subsequent neutralization of the distant Iroquois through diplomacy led to a loss of interest in military preparedness.

At present there is too little evidence to permit an evaluation of the tenuous but indisputable relationship between English military experiences in Ireland and developments in Virginia.[1] Insufficient evidence also makes it very difficult to determine whether what happened in Virginia significantly influenced the establishment of other Anglo-American paramilitary institutions.[2] Yet it seems highly unlikely that the successes of the Virginia militia could have failed to impress the men who sponsored and directed English overseas activities during the first half of the seventeenth century. It seems far more reasonable to assume that the founders of Plymouth and Massachusetts Bay and all the colonies that followed were more inclined to settle on a simple, inexpensive, and familiar paramilitary system for their security because of the example of the Old Dominion. Englishmen in Virginia demonstrated that an institution that was moribund in the Old World could be revitalized in the New. In so doing they helped to shape the course of future events.

1. New information on this relationship recently has been unearthed; see Noel Hume, *Martin's Hundred*, 234–37.

2. Good literature in this field is scarce. The place to begin is Shy, "New Look at Colonial Militia," 175–85; the best brief account of a single militia probably is Leach, "Military System of Plymouth Colony," 342–64. Additional studies are listed in the bibliography.

Bibliography

PRIMARY SOURCES

MANUSCRIPTS

Additional Manuscripts. British Library, London.
Blathwayt Papers. Huntington Library, San Marino, California.
Blathwayt, William. Papers. Research Center, Colonial Williamsburg Foundation, Williamsburg, Virginia.
Colonial Office Series. Public Record Office, London.
Coventry, Sir Henry. Papers. Longleat House, England.
Effingham, Baron Howard. Papers. Library of Congress, Washington, D.C.
State Papers. Public Record Office, London.
Virginia County Records. Virginia State Library, Richmond.

PUBLISHED WORKS

"Acts of the Generall Assembly, Jan. 6, 1639/40." *William and Mary Quarterly*, 2nd ser., IV (1924), 16–35, 145–62.

Acts of the Privy Council of England: Colonial Series, 1613–1680. Hereford, 1908.

"Acts, Orders and Resolutions of the General Assembly of Virginia: At Sessions of March 1643–1646." *Virginia Magazine of History and Biography*, XXII (1915), 225–55.

Ames, Susie M., ed. *County Court Records of Accomack-Northampton, Virginia, 1632–1640*. Washington, 1954.

———, ed. *County Court Records of Accomack-Northampton, Virginia, 1640–1645*. Charlottesville, 1973.

Andrews, Charles M., ed. *Narratives of the Insurrections, 1675–1690*. New York, 1915.

Arber, Edward, and A. G. Bradley, eds. *Travels and Works of Captain John Smith*. 2 vols. Edinburgh, 1910.

"The Aspinwall Papers." Massachusetts Historical Society *Collections*, 4th ser., IX (1871), 1–187.

"Attacks by the Dutch on the Virginia Fleet in Hampton Roads in 1667." *Virginia Magazine of History and Biography*, IV (1897), 229–45.

Barbour, Philip L., ed. *The Jamestown Voyages Under the First Charter, 1606–1609: Documents relating to the foundation of Jamestown and the history of the Jamestown colony up to the departure of Captain John Smith . . . early in October, 1609*. 2 vols. Cambridge, 1969.

Beverley, Robert. *The History and Present State of Virginia*. London, 1705.

Billings, Warren M., ed. "Some Acts Not in Hening's *Statutes*: The Acts of Assembly, April 1652, November 1652, and July 1653." *Virginia Magazine of History and Biography*, LXXXIII (1975), 22–76.

Birch, Thomas, ed. *The Court and Times of Charles the First*. 2 vols. London, 1848.

Brown, Alexander. *The First Republic in America*. Boston, 1898.

———. *The Genesis of the United States*. 2 vols. New York, 1890.

Brown, William H., et al., eds. *Archives of Maryland*. Baltimore, 1883–.

Clifford, Lewis, III, ed. "Some Recently Discovered Extracts from the Lost Minutes of the Virginia Council and General Court, 1642–1645." *William and Mary Quarterly*, 2nd ser., XX (1940), 62–78.

Davis, Richard B., ed. *William Fitzhugh and His Chesapeake World, 1676–1701: The Fitzhugh Letters and Other Documents*. Chapel Hill, 1963.

"Extracts from Proceedings of the House of Burgesses of Virginia, 1652–1661." *Virginia Magazine of History and Biography*, VIII (1901), 386–97.

Fausz, J. Frederick, and Jon Kukla, eds. "A Letter of Advice to the Governor of Virginia, 1624." *William and Mary Quarterly*, 3rd ser., XXXIV (1977), 104–29.

Force, Peter, ed. *Tracts and Other Papers, Relating Principally to the Origin, Settlement, and Progress of the Colonies in North America, from the Discovery of the Country to the Year 1776*. 4 vols. Washington, 1836–46.

Frank, Joseph. "News from Virginny, 1644." *Virginia Magazine of History and Biography*, LXV (1957), 84–87.

"Good Newes from Virginia, 1623." *William and Mary Quarterly*, 3rd ser., V (1948), 353–58.

Hamor, Ralph. *A True Discourse of the Present State of Virginia*. Richmond, 1957.

Hartwell, Henry, James Blair, and Edward Chilton. *The Present State of Virginia, and the College*. Edited by Hunter D. Farish. Charlottesville, 1964.

Hening, William W., ed. *The Statutes at Large; Being a Collection of All the Laws of Virginia, from the First Session of the Legislature, in the Year 1619*. 13 vols. Richmond, 1810–23.

Herrman, Augustine, cart. *Virginia and Maryland As it is Planted and Inhabited this present Year 1670*. London, 1673.

Jester, Annie L., and Martha W. Hiden, comps. and eds. *Adventurers of Purse and Person: Virginia, 1607–1625*. Princeton, 1956.

Johnson, Robert C., ed. "Virginia in 1632." *Virginia Magazine of History and Biography*, LXV (1957), 458–66.

Kingsbury, Susan M., ed. *The Records of the Virginia Company of London*. 4 vols. Washington, 1906–35.

McIlwaine, H. R., ed. *Legislative Journals of the Council of Colonial Virginia*. 3 vols. Richmond, 1918–19.

———, ed. *Minutes of the Council and General Court of Colonial Virginia, 1622–1632, 1670–1676*. Richmond, 1924.

McIlwaine, H. R., and W. L. Hall, eds. *Executive Journals of the Council of Colonial Virginia, 1680–1754*. 5 vols. Richmond, 1925–45.

McIlwaine, H. R., and J. P. Kennedy, eds. *Journals of the House of Burgesses of Virginia, 1619–1776*. 13 vols. Richmond, 1905–15.
Percy, George. "'A Trewe Relacyon,' Virginia from 1609 to 1612." *Tyler's Quarterly Historical and Genealogical Magazine*, III (1922), 259–82.
Purchas, Samuel. *Hakluytus Posthumus, or Purchas His Pilgrimes*. 20 vols. Glasgow, 1905–1907.
Rolfe, John. *A True Relation of the State of Virginia Lefte by Sir Thomas Dale Knight in May Last 1616*. Charlottesville, 1971.
Spotswood, Alexander. *The Official Letters of Alexander Spotswood, Lieutenant-Governor of Virginia, 1710–1722*. 2 vols. Richmond, 1882–85.
Strachey, William. *For the Colony in Virginea Britannia. Lawes Divine, Morall and Martiall*. Edited by David H. Flaherty. Charlottesville, 1969.
———. *The Historie of Travell into Virginia Britania*. Edited by Louis B. Wright and Virginia Freund. London, 1953.
Tinling, Marion, ed. *The Correspondence of the Three William Byrds of Westover, Virginia, 1684–1776*. 2 vols. Charlottesville, 1977.
Tyler, Lyon G., ed. *Narratives of Early Virginia, 1606–1625*. New York, 1907.
Virginia Gazette, February 23, 1769.
Washburn, Wilcomb E., ed. "Sir William Berkeley's 'A History of Our Miseries.'" *William and Mary Quarterly*, 3rd ser., XIV (1957), 403–13.
Wright, Irene A., ed. "Spanish Policy Toward Virginia, 1606–1612." *American Historical Review*, XXV (1920), 448–79.

SECONDARY SOURCES

Andrews, Charles M. *The Colonial Period of American History*. 4 vols. New Haven, 1934–38.
Bailyn, Bernard. "Politics and Social Structure in Virginia." In *Seventeenth-Century America: Essays in Colonial History*, edited by James M. Smith. Chapel Hill, 1959.
Barbour, Philip L. *The Three Worlds of Captain John Smith*. Boston, 1964.
Beeler, John. *Warfare in Feudal Europe, 730–1200*. Ithaca, 1971.
Billings, Warren M. "The Causes of Bacon's Rebellion: Some Suggestions." *Virginia Magazine of History and Biography*, LXXVIII (1970), 409–35.
———. "English Legal Literature as a Source of Law and Legal Practice for Seventeenth-Century Virginia." *Virginia Magazine of History and Biography*, LXXXVIII (1974), 403–16.
———. "The Growth of Political Institutions in Virginia, 1634 to 1676." *William and Mary Quarterly*, 3rd ser., XXXI (1974), 225–42.
———, ed. *The Old Dominion in the Seventeenth Century: A Documentary History of Virginia, 1606–1689*. Chapel Hill, 1975.
Blok, Petrus J. *History of the People of the Netherlands*. 4 vols. New York, 1898–1912.
Boddie, John B. *Colonial Surry*. Richmond, 1948.

———. *Seventeenth Century Isle of Wight County, Virginia*. Chicago, 1938.

Boynton, Lindsay. *The Elizabethan Militia, 1558–1638*. London, 1967.

Breen, T. H. "A Changing Labor Force and Race Relations in Virginia, 1660–1710." *Journal of Social History*, VII (1973), 3–25.

———. "English Origins and New World Development: The Case of the Covenanted Militia in Seventeenth-Century Massachusetts." *Past and Present*, LVII (1972), 76–96.

———. "Looking Out for Number One: Conflicting Cultural Values in Early Seventeenth Century Virginia." *South Atlantic Quarterly*, LXXVIII (1979), 342–60.

Breen, T. H., and Stephen Innes. *"Myne Owne Ground": Race and Freedom on Virginia's Eastern Shore, 1640–1676*. Oxford, 1980.

Bruce, Philip A. *Economic History of Virginia in the Seventeenth Century*. 2 vols. New York, 1895.

———. *Institutional History of Virginia in the Seventeenth Century*. 2 vols. New York, 1910.

Campbell, Charles. *History of the Colony and Ancient Dominion of Virginia*. Philadelphia, 1860.

Canny, Nicholas P. *The Elizabethan Conquest of Ireland: A Pattern Established, 1565–1576*. New York, 1976.

Carr, Lois G., and Russell R. Menard. "Immigration and Opportunity: The Freedman in Early Colonial Maryland." In *The Chesapeake in the Seventeenth Century: Essays on Anglo-American Society*, edited by Thad W. Tate and David L. Ammerman. Chapel Hill, 1979.

Carr, Lois G., and Lorena S. Walsh. "The Planter's Wife: The Experience of White Women in Seventeenth-Century Maryland." *William and Mary Quarterly*, 3rd ser., XXXIV (1977), 542–71.

Colden, Cadwallader. *The History of the Five Indian Nations Depending on the Province of New-York in America*. Ithaca, 1958.

Cole, David. "A Brief Outline of the South Carolina Colonial Militia System." South Carolina Historical Association *Proceedings* (1955), 14–23.

Cotter, John L. *Archeological Excavations at Jamestown National Historical Park and Jamestown National Historic Site, Virginia*. Washington, 1958.

Craven, Wesley F. *The Colonies in Transition, 1660–1713*. New York, 1968.

———. *Dissolution of the Virginia Company: The Failure of a Colonial Experiment*. Oxford, 1932.

———. "Indian Policy in Early Virginia." *William and Mary Quarterly*, 3rd ser., I (1944), 65–82.

———. *The Southern Colonies in the Seventeenth Century, 1607–1689*. Baton Rouge, 1949.

———. *White, Red, and Black: The Seventeenth-Century Virginian*. Charlottesville, 1971.

Cruickshank, C. G. *Elizabeth's Army*. Oxford, 1966.

Davis, Richard B. *Intellectual Life in the Colonial South, 1585–1763*. 3 vols. Knoxville, 1978.

DeValinger, Leon. *Colonial Military Organization in Delaware, 1638–1776*. Wilmington, 1938.

Diamond, Sigmund. "From Organization to Society: Virginia in the Seventeenth Century." *American Journal of Sociology*, LXIII (1958), 457–75.

Earle, Carville E. "Environment, Disease, and Mortality in Early Virginia." In *The Chesapeake in the Seventeenth Century: Essays on Anglo-American Society*, edited by Thad W. Tate and David L. Ammerman. Chapel Hill, 1979.

Eccles, W. J. "The Social, Economic, and Political Significance of the Military Establishment in New France." *Canadian Historical Review*, LII (1971), 1–21.

Falls, Cyril. *Elizabeth's Irish Wars*. London, 1950.

Fausz, J. Frederick. "Fighting 'Fire' with Firearms: The Anglo-Powhatan Arms Race in Early Virginia." *American Indian Culture and Research Journal*, III (1979), 33–50.

———. "George Thorpe, Nemattanew, and the Powhatan Uprising of 1622." *Virginia Cavalcade*, XXIX (1979), 111–17.

———. "The Powhatan Uprising of 1622: A Historical Study of Ethnocentrism and Cultural Conflict." Ph.D. dissertation, College of William and Mary, 1977.

Ferguson, Alice L. "The Susquehannock Fort on Piscataway Creek." *Maryland Historical Magazine*, XXXVI (1941), 1–9.

Ferling, John E. *A Wilderness of Miseries: War and Warriors in Early America*. Westport, 1980.

Forman, Henry C. *Jamestown and St. Mary's: Buried Cities of Romance*. Baltimore, 1938.

French, Allen. "The Arms and Military Training of Our Colonizing Ancestors." Massachusetts Historical Society *Proceedings*, LXVII (1941–44), 3–21.

Friedman, Lawrence J., and Arthur H. Shaffer. "The Conway Robinson Notes and Seventeenth-Century Virginia." *Virginia Magazine of History and Biography*, LXXVIII (1970), 259–67.

Geyl, Pieter. *The Netherlands in the Seventeenth Century: Part II, 1648–1715*. London, 1964.

Harrison, Fairfax. *Landmarks of Old Prince William: A Study of Origins in Northern Virginia*. Berryville, 1964.

Hecht, Irene W. D. "The Virginia Muster of 1624/5 as a Source for Demographic History." *William and Mary Quarterly*, 3rd ser., XXX (1973), 65–92.

Hollister, C. Warren. *Anglo-Saxon Military Institutions on the Eve of the Norman Conquest*. Oxford, 1962.

———. *The Military Organization of Norman England*. Oxford, 1965.

Hunt, George T. *The Wars of the Iroquois: A Study in Intertribal Trade Relations*. Madison, 1940.
Jabbs, Theodore H. "The South Carolina Colonial Militia, 1663–1733." Ph.D. dissertation, University of North Carolina, 1973.
Kelly, Kevin P. "'In dispers'd Country Plantations': Settlement Patterns in Seventeenth-Century Surry County, Virginia." In *The Chesapeake in the Seventeenth Century: Essays on Anglo-American Society*, edited by Thad W. Tate and David L. Ammerman. Chapel Hill, 1979.
Land, Aubrey C., et al., eds. *Law, Society, and Politics in Early Maryland*. Baltimore, 1977.
Leach, Douglas E. *Arms for Empire: A Military History of the British Colonies in North America, 1607–1763*. New York, 1973.
———. "The Military System of Plymouth Colony." *New England Quarterly*, XXIV (1951), 342–64.
Lewis, Michael. "Armada Guns." *Mariner's Mirror*, XXVIII (1942), 41–73.
Lurie, Nancy O. "Indian Cultural Adjustment to European Civilization." In *Seventeenth-Century America: Essays in Colonial History*, edited by James M. Smith. Chapel Hill, 1959.
McCary, Ben C. *Indians in Seventeenth-Century Virginia*. Charlottesville, 1957.
Malone, Patrick M. "Indian and English Military Systems in New England in the Seventeenth Century." Ph.D. dissertation, Brown University, 1971.
Marcus, Richard H. "The Militia of Colonial Connecticut, 1639–1775: An Institutional Study." Ph.D. dissertation, University of Colorado, 1965.
Menard, Russell R. "A Note on Chesapeake Tobacco Prices, 1618–1660." *Virginia Magazine of History and Biography*, LXXXIV (1976), 401–10.
Middleton, Arthur P. "The Chesapeake Convoy System, 1662–1763." *William and Mary Quarterly*, 3rd ser., III (1946), 182–207.
———. *Tobacco Coast: A Maritime History of Chesapeake Bay in the Colonial Era*. Newport News, 1953.
Millar, David R. "The Militia, the Army, and Independency in Colonial Massachusetts." Ph.D. dissertation, Cornell University, 1967.
Miller, John. "The Militia and the Army in the Reign of James II." *Historical Journal*, XVI (1973), 659–79.
Mook, Maurice A. "The Aboriginal Population of Tidewater Virginia." *American Anthropologist*, XLIV (1944), 193–208.
Mooney, James. "The Powhatan Confederacy, Past and Present." *American Anthropologist*, IX (1907), 128–52.
Morgan, Edmund S. *American Slavery, American Freedom: The Ordeal of Colonial Virginia*. New York, 1975.
———. "The First American Boom: Virginia 1618 to 1630." *William and Mary Quarterly*, 3rd ser., XXVIII (1971), 169–98.
———. "Headrights and Head Counts: A Review Article." *Virginia Magazine of History and Biography*, LXXX (1972), 361–71.

Morton, Louis. "The Origins of American Military Policy." *Military Affairs,* XXII (1958), 75–82.
Morton, Richard L. *Colonial Virginia.* 2 vols. Chapel Hill, 1960.
Nash, Gary B. "The Image of the Indian in the Southern Colonial Mind." *William and Mary Quarterly,* 3rd ser., XXIX (1972), 197–230.
Noel Hume, Ivor. *Martin's Hundred.* New York, 1982.
Peterson, Harold L. *Arms and Armor in Colonial America.* Harrisburg, 1956.
Poole, Austin L., ed. *Medieval England.* 2 vols. Oxford, 1958.
Powell, William S. "Aftermath of the Massacre: The First Indian War, 1622–1632." *Virginia Magazine of History and Biography,* LXVI (1958), 44–75.
Powicke, Michael. *Military Obligation in Medieval England: A Study in Liberty and Duty.* Oxford, 1962.
Quinn, David B. *North America from Earliest Discovery to First Settlements: The Norse Voyages to 1612.* New York, 1977.
Radabaugh, Jack S. "The Militia of Colonial Massachusetts." *Military Affairs,* XXVIII (1954), 1–18.
Rainbolt, John C. "The Alteration in the Relationship Between Leadership and Constituents in Virginia, 1660 to 1720." *William and Mary Quarterly,* 3rd ser., XXVII (1970), 410–34.
———. "A New Look at Stuart 'Tyranny': The Crown's Attack on the Virginia Assembly, 1676–1689." *Virginia Magazine of History and Biography,* LXXV (1967), 387–406.
Roberts, Michael. *The Military Revolution, 1560–1660.* Belfast, 1956.
Robinson, W. Stitt. "Tributary Indians in Colonial Virginia." *Virginia Magazine of History and Biography,* LXVII (1959), 49–64.
Rutman, Darrett B. "A Militant New World, 1607–1640." Ph.D. dissertation, University of Virginia, 1959.
———. "The Virginia Company and Its Military Regime." In *The Old Dominion: Essays for Thomas Perkins Abernethy,* edited by Darrett B. Rutman. Charlottesville, 1964.
Scisco, Louis D. "Evolution of Colonial Militia in Maryland." *Maryland Historical Magazine,* XXXV (1940), 166–77.
Shea, William L. "The First American Militia." *Military Affairs,* XLVI (1982), 15–18.
———. "Virginia at War, 1644–1646." *Military Affairs,* XLI (1977), 142–47.
Shy, John W. "A New Look at Colonial Militia." *William and Mary Quarterly,* 3rd ser., XX (1963), 175–85.
Smail, R. C. "Art of War." In *Medieval England,* edited by Austin L. Poole. Oxford, 1958.
Smart, George K. "Private Libraries in Colonial Virginia." *American Literature,* X (1938), 24–52.
Smith, James M., ed. *Seventeenth-Century America: Essays in Colonial History.* Chapel Hill, 1959.
Stith, William. *The History of the First Discovery and Settlement of Vir-*

ginia: Being an Essay Towards a General History of this Colony. Williamsburg, 1747.

Tate, Thad W., and David L. Ammerman, eds. *The Chesapeake in the Seventeenth Century: Essays on Anglo-American Society*. Chapel Hill, 1979.

Thompson, Gladys S. *Lords Lieutenants in the Sixteenth Century: A Study in Tudor Local Administration*. London, 1923.

Thornton, J. Mills, III. "The Thrusting Out of Governor Harvey: A Seventeenth-Century Rebellion." *Virginia Magazine of History and Biography*, LXXVI (1968), 11–26.

Trelease, Allen W. *Indian Affairs in Colonial New York: The Seventeenth Century*. Ithaca, 1960.

Vaughan, Alden T. "'Expulsion of the Salvages': English Policy and the Virginia Massacre of 1622." *William and Mary Quarterly*, 3rd ser., XXXV (1978), 57–84.

Wallace, Anthony F. C. *The Death and Rebirth of the Seneca*. New York, 1970.

Washburn, Wilcomb E. *The Governor and the Rebel: A History of Bacon's Rebellion in Virginia*. Chapel Hill, 1957.

———. "Governor Berkeley and King Philip's War." *New England Quarterly*, XXX (1957), 363–77.

———. *Virginia Under Charles I and Cromwell, 1625–1660*. Charlottesville, 1957.

Webb, Stephen S. "Army and Empire: English Garrison Government in Britain and America, 1569 to 1763." *William and Mary Quarterly*, 3rd ser., XXXIV (1977), 1–31.

Wertenbaker, Thomas J. *Torchbearer of the Revolution: The Story of Bacon's Rebellion and Its Leader*. Princeton, 1940.

Western, J. R. *The English Militia in the Eighteenth Century: The Story of a Political Issue, 1660–1802*. London, 1965.

Wheeler, E. Milton. "Development and Organization of North Carolina Militia." *North Carolina Historical Review*, XLI (1964), 307–23.

Wilson, Charles. *Profit and Power: A Study of England and the Dutch Wars*. London, 1957.

Wright, Louis B. *The First Gentlemen of Virginia: Intellectual Qualities of the Early Colonial Ruling Class*. San Marino, 1940.

Yonge, Samuel H. *The Site of Old "James Towne," 1607–1698: A Brief Historical and Topographical Sketch of the First American Metropolis*. Richmond, 1907.

Index